What Your Colleagues Are Saying . . .

...entfer is the 21st-century Madeline Hunter! Dr. Lentfer's CALM approach makes so much sense. This book ...e required reading for all first-year teachers who often struggle with classroom management. Finally a ...-step approach that helps to diffuse classroom disruptions while allowing teachers to teach and students to ...i. Classrooms can become kind and caring learning environments that have high expectations and respect all students.

Pamela J. Cohn, Executive ~~Director~~ ...hool
Support an~~d~~ ... ...ools

CALM Classroom Management is critical to teaching success. The author has ... to learning from mistakes, digging into the research, engaging in reflection, ana... ...er in the area of classroom management. This book applies a practical, no-nonsense, ...ed approach that includes research-based case studies and activities to help teachers and administr... ...successful.

Nancy A. Edick, Lois G. Roskens Dean, College of Education,
University of Nebraska Omaha

Dr. Lentfer's book on classroom management reaches a broad audience. Her philosophy of CALM (Communication, Accountability, Leadership, and Motivation) allows educators to see and relate practical strategies teachers can implement tomorrow.

Kim Campbell, Proud Middle School Teacher/AMLE Consultant/
SOAR Coordinator/Dean of Students,
Hopkins School District

CALM Management is a simple, yet effective way for teachers to establish a positive learning environment. Teachers are able to establish a respectful classroom by using the proactive methods in the CALM Management Program. This step-by-step approach empowers students through choices and accountability. This is a must-read for new teachers!

Jim Sutfin, Superintendent,
Millard Public Schools

Dr. Lentfer's CALM Management Program is the answer to every teacher's biggest wish: to have a classroom environment where every single student can experience success. She provides simple, clear, and proven techniques for classroom management, with examples from real classrooms, at every level of schooling. Every teacher needs a copy of this book, new and veteran alike!

Ferial Pearson, College of Education,
University of Nebraska Omaha

This is one of the best classroom management books that I have read. The CALM management tools will help all educators at any stages of their careers. The activities, real-world examples, and reflection questions made the content interactive and meaningful. This book is an invaluable resource for teachers at all levels of their careers!

Susan M. Swearer, Willa Cather Professor of
Educational Psychology,
University of Nebraska—Lincoln

Everyone is seeking the one answer regarding classroom management. The truth is, there is no one perfect answer. However, staying CALM, building relationships, using humor, and setting realistic expectations can help you as an educator. This book explores how critical it is to be proactive and thoughtful in your classroom management. Next time things get so crazy in your classroom that you want to set your hair on fire, remember to stay calm—wigs are expensive!

Jack Berckemeyer, Presenter and Author of *Taming of the Team*,
Berckemeyer Consulting Group

Filled with actionable and adaptable strategies for all grade levels, this text is a comprehensive guide for establishing a classroom environment where all students can thrive. A valuable and explicit resource for teachers new to the profession, as well as career educators wishing to reset their classroom management process and procedures.

Melissa Chalupnik, Director of Professional Learning,
Council Bluffs Community Schools

This is a great how-to book that provides excellent strategies and tools to create a smooth-functioning classroom leading to increased instructional time and student learning. For the novice teacher, it offers many procedures that can be easily implemented into a classroom management framework. For the experienced teacher, it provides ideas that can be applied, adapted, and integrated into their existing classroom management model. This is a valuable resource for all teachers in PreK–12 school settings.

Janice Garnett, University of Nebraska Omaha, Instructor,
Retired Assistant Superintendent, Omaha Public Schools

Vicki has outlined a logical road map not only to address behavior, but change the narrative regarding classroom management to reflect a shift in mindset that replaces irrational responses with positive choices that are effective in keeping the focus on student learning.

Marlena Gross-Taylor, Founder of #EduGladiators,
Social Commerce Entrepreneur, Author, Speaker, EdLeader, AMLE Expert,
MarlenaTaylor.com

If I had this book my first year of teaching, I would have floundered less and my students would have learned more! Dr. Lentfer does a thorough job of breaking down classroom management. The book is full of concrete examples for elementary, middle school, and high school teachers, thoroughly explaining the steps to establishing the learning environment that typically takes teachers years to achieve.

Tony Vincent,
LearninginHand.com

As an ESL teacher educator, I am grateful that Dr. Lentfer's CALM Management Program addresses the needs of diverse learners. With their strong focus on building relationships, the CALM management strategies will empower teacher candidates, experienced teachers, teacher educators, and most important, students of all ages, languages, and cultural backgrounds.

Sandra Rodriguez-Arroyo,
Associate Professor of Education, ESL/Bilingual Education and Literacy,
University of Nebraska Omaha

Keep CALM and Teach

Keep CALM and Teach

Empowering K–12 Learners With Positive Classroom Management Routines

Victoria Lentfer

A joint publication with the Association for Middle Level Education (AMLE)

CORWIN
A SAGE Publishing Company

AMLE

FOR INFORMATION:

Corwin

A SAGE Company

2455 Teller Road

Thousand Oaks, California 91320

(800) 233-9936

www.corwin.com

SAGE Publications Ltd.

1 Oliver's Yard

55 City Road

London EC1Y 1SP

United Kingdom

SAGE Publications India Pvt. Ltd.

B 1/I 1 Mohan Cooperative Industrial Area

Mathura Road, New Delhi 110 044

India

SAGE Publications Asia-Pacific Pte. Ltd.

3 Church Street

#10-04 Samsung Hub

Singapore 049483

Acquisitions Editor: Ariel Curry

Development Editor: Desirée A. Bartlett

Editorial Assistant: Jessica Vidal

Production Editor: Tori Mirsadjadi

Copy Editor: Talia Greenberg

Typesetter: C&M Digitals (P) Ltd.

Proofreader: Sally Jaskold

Indexer: Beth Nauman-Montana

Cover Designer: Scott Van Atta

Marketing Manager: Brian Grimm

Printed in the United States of America

ISBN: 978-1-5063-9776-4

This book is printed on acid-free paper.

SUSTAINABLE FORESTRY INITIATIVE

Certified Chain of Custody
Promoting Sustainable Forestry
www.sfiprogram.org
SFI-01268

SFI label applies to text stock

18 19 20 21 22 10 9 8 7 6 5 4 3 2 1

Contents

Preface

I have worked with some phenomenal teachers, and I have worked with some who struggled with classroom management. I was one of those who struggled. My first year I would go home exhausted, my tongue swollen from talking so much, and frustrated because I had been reacting to student behavior all day. I wasn't enjoying myself, and I was sure my students held the same sentiment.

That summer I was determined to make a change. My ultimate goal was to have a calm, peaceful classroom. I worked long hours creating a plan. I noticed a couple of tendencies where I was reactive in addressing student behavior, and my challenges often centered on breakdowns in communication. The next year I was prepared. I developed and implemented my strategies with great success. Teachers began to notice a change, particularly in how calm I was throughout the day. New teachers wanted to know my secret.

This was the beginning of the CALM Management techniques. CALM stands for Communication, Accountability, Leadership, and Motivation. Communication because I wanted to develop my skills and my students' skills in communicating in a more clear, concise, and respectful manner. Accountability because I needed a system that would develop students as independent thinkers and that would make them accountable for their behavior and academic success. Leadership because it's important for teachers and students to develop respectful relationships and to cocreate a culture of support, encouragement, and empowerment. And finally, motivation is key to inspiring a calm classroom where innovation and creativity flourish.

When I developed CALM, it did not mean all students would be quiet, sitting in rows and being compliant. Compliance does not equal engagement. A CALM classroom may look and sound different every day. Yes, there may be days when students are quiet while working in groups or independently. But there also may be times when the classroom appears chaotic. However, the students are engaged in group activities. Their voices are raised because they are talking about their projects, exchanging ideas, and able to work as a team. Both examples are appropriate. Quiet and chaotic are part of CALM; the key element is *engagement*.

> Quiet and chaotic are part of CALM; the key element is *engagement*.

This book isn't just about why it's important to have a well-managed classroom. It gives the *how*. As educators, we are fairly well versed in the importance of having good classroom management skills; this book gives you actual strategies and tools you can implement the next day. They apply to any level for Grades K–12. There are communication models for teachers and students, models for collaborative work groups, and models that teach students how to be respectful to themselves and their classmates.

Developing classroom management skills and techniques that work can be extremely challenging for classroom teachers, especially new teachers. The purpose for this book is to provide educators with *proactive* strategies that address behavior management with all students. The proactive strategies consist of teaching behavior expectations that are primarily addressed within the first month of school.

CALM is centered on creating a culture of community, of developing relationships, respect, and trust by engaging in respectful conversations. The communication models for teachers and students are shown throughout the book and are in response to the frequently asked question: *What do you say when* _____ [insert inappropriate behavior]*?* All student and teacher names have been changed to protect their privacy.

It is my hope that the CALM Management strategies offered in this book will provide a solid reference for teachers in developing a classroom that centers on positive behavior expectations, respect, building relationships, and trust.

FIGURE 0.1   CALM Management

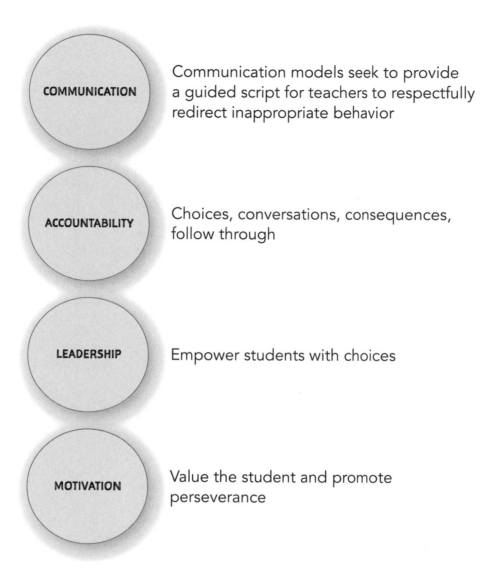

COMMUNICATION   Communication models seek to provide a guided script for teachers to respectfully redirect inappropriate behavior

ACCOUNTABILITY   Choices, conversations, consequences, follow through

LEADERSHIP   Empower students with choices

MOTIVATION   Value the student and promote perseverance

Acknowledgments

I would like to dedicate this book to my parents, to Charlotte, and to Patty. Thank you for all of your love and support.

I also would like to acknowledge all of my former and current teachers, colleagues, and students. I will forever be grateful for all of the experiences and life lessons you have taught me, and without each of you, this book would not have been possible.

Publisher's Acknowledgments

Corwin gratefully acknowledges the contributions of the following reviewers:

Melissa Cast-Brede, Professor
University of Nebraska Omaha
Omaha, Nebraska

Frank Chiki, Classroom Teacher K/1
Alice King Community School
Albuquerque, New Mexico

LaVonda Cooper-Smith, Vice Principal
Bahamas Academy of Seventh-day Adventists
Nassau, The Bahamas

Katina Keener, Principal
Achilles Elementary
Hayes, Virginia

Courtney Pawol, First Grade Teacher
Stephenson Elementary
Portland, Oregon

Michelle Strom, Language Arts
Fort Riley Middle School
Fort Riley, Kansas

About the Author

Dr. Victoria Lentfer is an education instructor at the University of Nebraska Omaha. She teaches classroom management and middle level courses. She is an educational consultant and founder of the CALM Classroom Management Program, which is a comprehensive behavior management and teacher leader program that provides communication models to guide teachers and students to an inclusive and productive classroom. She has more than 20 years of experience in providing instructional support and teaching at both the middle and high school urban districts, and extensive work with incarcerated youth. Victoria has also been a Trailblazer Leader and keynote speaker for the Association of Middle Level Education (AMLE).

1 The CALM Management Program

How I Got From There to Here

I need to write letters of apology to all of my students, parents, and colleagues from my first year of teaching. I need to write letters because my voice was exhausted from all of the aggressive prompting I had to do to get students to listen to me. Whatever strategy I tried fell on deaf ears. But the problem was not my students' hearing; it was my lesson plans. My lesson plans were so well written and detailed they could have taught a cactus how to survive in the rainforest. But they weren't connecting with the students. As soon as I began delivering my lessons, I found some students bored, some wired. Where was I going wrong?

On the last day of school at 3:00 p.m. I marched down to my principal's office, shut the door, and began to cry. It was a frustrated, heavy-breathing, messy cry. I couldn't catch my breath and thought, "This is it—I'm going to die in my principal's office."

My principal was gracious with her time and a bit amused as I kept going on about how I was a damn good teacher. I'm not sure who I was trying to convince more—her or myself. I blamed the temperature in my room, the cafeteria ladies, and the president of the United States (POTUS). The POTUS was my principal's breaking point. To my surprise, I saw her eyes well with tears—not of anger or sorrow, but laughter. I couldn't believe it. As she wiped her tears, she smiled and calmly stated that I would just have to come back next year and start over. She politely pointed out that I had two and a half months to get myself together, and with that, she showed me the door.

Taking my principal's advice, I spent that summer conducting a task analysis on my teaching. It was brutal at times, but necessary. In order to start anew, I had to learn from the past, leave it in the past, and move forward. First, I wrote down everything that went wrong in my classroom, from failed lesson plans to the failed interactions between me and the students. I then made two lists; one list consisted of what I didn't want to see or hear in my classroom, and the other consisted of what I did want to see and hear. I then identified specific behaviors that would trigger a negative response from me and behaviors that would trigger negative responses from the students.

The deeper I got into my task analysis, the more it became clear to me that my first year of teaching lacked communication, assessment, leadership, and motivation.

Reflecting on the poor communication in my classroom, I realized several things: (a) I hadn't gotten to know my students (lack of relationship building); (b) I didn't understand why my students hesitated to share their ideas (lack of trust building); (c) words and actions did not reflect kindness (lack of respect); and (d) my lessons lacked direction and clear expectations (lack of clarity).

Relationships. Relationships are the cornerstone of a well-managed classroom. Had I paid more attention to relationship building, I could have circumvented a lot of chaos.

Trust. If I didn't have a relationship with my students, how could I expect them to trust me? Trust and relationships go hand in hand.

Respect. I found that my students and I had different views and experiences regarding respect. Often, the interpretation of the meaning of respect was one of the most disguised causes of disputes in the classroom. Teachers and students need to build a working definition of respect together through ongoing dialogue.

Clarity. Lesson directions were unclear. I assumed the students understood what I expected of them, even though I hadn't communicated the learning intentions and success criteria.

In addition, I realized that in order to successfully build relationships, gain trust, and maintain a respectful classroom, my demeanor needed to remain CALM. Students will respond and mirror the teacher's demeanor. If they sense your anxiety, they will feel anxiety as well.

> Students will respond and mirror the teacher's demeanor. If they sense your anxiety, they will feel anxiety as well.

A lot of good came from this task-analysis exercise. Most significant, it made me determined to become a better teacher. I resolved to take the time to get to know my students. I would be a better colleague. I would strive to be a role model whom students would try to emulate. I resolved not to let a young child get the best of me. I would devise a plan that would enable me to be in control without being the center of action. I wanted the students to be the center of action. I would be on the side, encouraging them to make good choices.

Teach Content *and* Behavior

I decided I was going to approach behavior as I would content. Just as it would not be appropriate to write the quadratic formula on the whiteboard and expect students to know how to use it to solve a problem, so too it was not appropriate to ask students to "behave," "pay attention," "cooperate," and "participate" without breaking down what that means and showing what it looks like. Like content, lessons in classroom behavioral norms and participation need to be reiterated and reinforced over time. Not all students learn at the same pace. Some students will be able to display appropriate behaviors without a lot of prompting; others may take more re-teaching.

I knew that I had to earn students' trust before they would be willing to follow me. I strove to teach with love, kindness, and respect. My goal was to create an inclusive environment with a strong sense of community. The fun part of teaching was getting to learn about my students and, in turn, about other countries and cultures.

> Like content, lessons in classroom behavioral norms and participation need to be reiterated and reinforced over time.

My disastrous first year of teaching is a common story. First-year teachers experience a lot of failure, only to find themselves at the beginning of the second year a much more wise and fit teacher. My goal with this book is to make the first-year rite of passage as painless as possible for other new teachers. Ideally, after reading this book, new teachers will be able to apply these strategies so that their classroom will be calm and peaceful. Classrooms should provide an experience students look forward to having every day, where teachers enjoy teaching and students enjoy learning. A place full of laughter and joy. A place full of positive relationships, trust, respect, clear expectations, and high expectations.

As you begin the year or semester, you can incorporate behavior expectations during instruction. It is a matter of supporting, prompting, and reinforcing the behavior expectations throughout each lesson. As the students become more proficient in achieving the behavior expectations, the teacher will gradually progress to concentrating on instruction. It is designed to progress to expand the learning environment.

CALM Management

CALM Management is an inclusive, community approach to behavior focused on building relationships, community, behavior skills, and academic achievement. It offers skills and strategies based on defining respect that teachers can implement immediately. CALM is focused on being relaxed, not letting fear block you from being the best version of you. "CALM" itself is an acronym for four key approaches to behavior management:

- Communication
- Accountability
- Leadership
- Motivation

We'll discuss each of these briefly here, and then in more depth in Parts I–IV of the book.

Communication

There are many variables that go into having a well-managed classroom. There are engaging lesson plans, transitions, collaborative working groups, independent and partner work, procedures, consequences, and much more. But the one variable that is often overlooked is communication.

CALM provides teachers with communication models that are proactive, teaching students respect by defining it through words and actions. The Voice-Movement-Task Model (VMT) addresses specific areas that pose the greatest barrier to productive work groups. It presents behavior expectations prior to an activity as well as how to communicate clear and concise directions for completing the group work.

Communication has the potential to bridge the gap between a well-disciplined, productive classroom and a classroom that uses punitive measures to expel students without regard to teaching how to monitor their self-regulation. The art of communication involves clear, concise verbal and nonverbal expressions. Effective teacher communication can improve students' ability to synthesize and process information at a high level. In order to maintain a productive, safe learning environment for all learners it is essential to address best practices in communication.

Verbal Communication

Verbal communication is vital for enhancing relationships and plays a key role in the development of the whole child. Positive reinforcement can come in a multitude of forms such as: verbal reinforcers, effective praise, clear directions, simple requests, empathy, corrective feedback, and casual conversations. Verbal communication may involve words, spoken or written. We use verbal communication to inform or impart knowledge. Clarity is a key component of successful communication. Often, this is the area in which we as educators need to reflect on our practices in articulating our thoughts in a more clear and concise manner.

Nonverbal Communication

Teacher–student communication is much more than explicit directions; it involves implicit directives, which are expressed through nonverbal interactions. Nonverbal messages reinforce what your words convey. They transmit your emotions, define relationships, and provide feedback. Being aware of the feedback you are giving students is critical in building their confidence to take academic risks in your classroom. In some cases, our nonverbal communication can be more important than the words we speak. Nonverbal messages are usually perceived as being less controlled than our verbal messages and therefore more reflective of our true feelings. In other words, actions speak louder than words.

Nonverbal communication may include:

- *Body movement:* head nod, hand gestures, arms crossed, hands on hips, proximity, shaking head in disapproval

- *Posture:* standing tall, shoulders back, slouched, inward bend

- *Eye contact:* trusting, kind, defensive staring, rolling eyes

- *Facial expressions:* smile, frown

Tone of Voice

In addition to practicing supportive verbal and nonverbal communication skills, teachers should be conscious of their tone of voice. Voice tone involves the inflection, rhythm, pitch, and rate of speech. It is not so much the words we say, but the manner in how we say them. Voice tone consists of energy and expressive speech. As adults, we have all been on the receiving end of a positive or negative voice tone from our parents, a former teacher, or even a stranger on the street. Just think about how you reacted to someone's voice tone when it was positive and when it was negative. When redirecting student behavior, your tone should convey empathy and understanding as well as assertiveness. *Remain CALM.*

It is unrealistic to think that teachers will never become angry. It is a natural, normal emotion that everyone experiences. While difficult to accomplish, being able to acquire a CALM demeanor is a worthy endeavor. A CALM demeanor enables you to remain in control over your reactions and responses and helps you to stay focused on the specific behavior you need to address. Remaining CALM allows you to teach and guide, and it does not follow the escalating cycles of anger and erratic behavior.

Maintaining a calm demeanor is a skill and an attitude that can be developed. You have to consciously choose to embrace the change. As with any change, it will take time and practice. Remember, a student's behavior is not a reflection of you; you cannot take their behavior personally. Remaining CALM places you in a position of control, and you are less likely to become vulnerable to argument or be manipulated by the student.

Practice the following to develop a calm disposition:

- *Pleasant tone.* Use a pleasant tone as often as possible.

- *Deep breath.* Take a few deep breaths to help calm yourself.

- *Honesty.* Let the student know you are upset right now: "I need a few minutes to gather my thoughts and we'll talk about this in a few minutes." You are modeling how to regain control of your emotions before having a conversation.

- *Rationale.* The Redirect Behavior Model (see Chapter 3) implicitly requires you to address the rationale. It also gives everyone a little time to calm their emotions. It provides the "why" for the situation.

- *Time.* Take a moment before you address the behavior. Do not be rushed.

Accountability

Accountability is at the heart of CALM Management. The idea is to promote students' awareness to display appropriate behavior, develop respectful behavior skills, and empower them through choice. When students are given choices, they are aware of the outcomes of both positive and negative choices. Their choices are reinforced with the idea that for every action there is a reaction; whether there is a positive or negative outcome depends on their decision.

The CALM Management methods of Positive Behavior Expectations (PBEs) and the Redirect Behavior Model (RBM) reinforce and strengthen accountability. They empower students to make the right choices and increase their ability to self-monitor their behavior. This accountability lays the foundation for productive collaborative work groups. We will explore how to create efficient and effective collaborative work groups and cultivate an environment of accountability in Chapter 5.

Leadership

The Leadership section focuses on developing teachers and students as leaders. You will find methods for assertively promoting your overall health and wellness. There will also be guided reflections to help you take a close look at teacher dispositions and how biases might affect your teaching practice.

The ultimate goal is to teach students to become independent thinkers. The Small-Group Interaction Model (discussed in Chapter 5) fosters an environment for students to collaborate in a supportive manner.

Students as leaders will learn how to communicate in a calm, assertive manner. Through participation in the Community Council (discussed in Chapter 8), students will hone their leadership skills by learning how to monitor the behavior and academics of their peers.

As a teacher leader in the classroom, you are going to be working hard, but that does not mean your students are going to be told what and how to do things all of the time. You are going to teach and lead students to make good choices and hold themselves accountable for their actions. This takes time and a ton of work. But in the end it is well worth the effort. Once you have established the culture of community in the classroom and teamwork, that's when the fun begins. You are going to teach them life skills to be able to work for one another and have a culture of responsibility and a strong work ethic.

Motivation

Once you have established a calm classroom where respect is the expectation and appropriate behavior is the norm, you will be able to try new strategies that inspire students to achieve. It is very common for teachers to have difficulty with the disengaged student. You will find methods for devising creative ideas that will jumpstart student motivation.

The CALM program is not a quick fix. It will take time to develop relationships and to build trust and respect between the teacher and students. But the time is well worth the effort. If you spend a considerable amount of time using the CALM methods during the first month of class, you will be able to be the guide on the side with confidence midway through your first semester. Keep in mind that if you approach behavior as you do content, each student will be able to display the key skills at their own pace.

> Keep in mind that if you approach behavior as you do content, each student will be able to display the key skills at their own pace.

Here are some additional considerations/strategies to implement along with CALM Management.

Proactive Measures

As a teacher I have attended many hours of professional development, some of them helpful. The best professional development sessions provided us with strategies linked to a strong rationale that we could implement immediately. Some sounded good, but they did not offer implementation guidance. For example, we had a series of sessions that addressed the need to empower our students, let them be in control of their learning. I walked away thinking, this sounds great, but they didn't tell us how. Do I go into my classroom and announce, "Today I am going to empower you to make good choices"? I knew that in order to empower my students I needed to implement proactive strategies to prepare them to become independent thinkers. This is when I began to develop strategies to gradually release the power from teacher to student.

Positive Reinforcements

I am a big believer in positively reinforcing appropriate behavior. Positive energy will compound over time with encouraging words and actions. I encourage my students as well as myself to be aware of their word choices. Positive words and actions have an impact that reaches far beyond the classroom walls. Positive energy is contagious. Making a conscientious effort to develop a positive work environment will aid in positive student interactions and help to develop a trusting, safe environment, which is crucial in developing strong relationships in the classroom.

Pacing

It is important to note that these strategies build upon one another. Pacing will be key to your success. All of the methods presented will not be able to be implemented immediately. Yes, there are strategies that can be implemented the next day, but the CALM method is a progression. As the book introduces new strategies, it is necessary for the educator to evaluate their students' behavior. Are they able to handle working with partners? Small groups? How do they conduct themselves during independent work time?

Start small and build upon your successes. Introduce partner work, progress to cooperative learning groups, and eventually you will be able to transition to a project-based learning approach. These methods take time to implement and time for students to understand the expectations and be able to display the appropriate behavior according to the classroom expectations. It's a progression in which the educator will need to be cognizant of gradually implementing all of the CALM methods. It takes time to establish the culture of your classroom, and all of these methods will work in unison to help establish a supportive community in your classroom and school.

Mastery of the CALM methods is a process. Pacing is also important in incorporating these methods. Novice teachers may not incorporate all the methods until their second year of teaching. The novice teacher within the first year should concentrate on mastering the Positive Behavior Expectations (PBEs), employing the Redirect Behavior Model (RBM) in a conversational style, and implementing the Voice-Movement-Task Model (VMT). These are the cornerstones of creating a calm, productive classroom. Year Two, the novice teacher may begin to employ the other methods discussed in the book, such as the Community Council (CC) and the Student Communication Model (SCM).

Learning Goals

The main objective for establishing a well-managed classroom is to provide an environment for students to enhance their academic skills. Learning goals are as much a part of classroom management as behavior goals. Learning goals can only begin to be achieved once the behavior goals have been established. Learning goals are what every teacher envisions. Once the students understand and are able to follow the behavior expectations, then the teacher is able to expand the learning environment and engage students in analyzing, synthesizing, and evaluating their progress. Well-managed classrooms provide a stable, supportive working community in which students can excel academically. Learning goals and behavior goals work together in unison to communicate the expectations necessary for students to achieve at their highest level.

> Learning goals are as much a part of classroom management as behavior goals.

Behavior Goals

Behavior goals will help to support the learning goals by providing a foundation for having a well-managed classroom. Teachers need to provide behavior goals in conjunction with learning goals and communicate these in a clear and concise manner. The goals will increase student success by creating a culture of high expectations and accountability. Academic and behavior goals create an orderly environment. Behavior goals will assist in paving the way for high-quality instruction to take place.

Summary

The CALM Management method is a comprehensive system. Mastery is a progression, so pace yourself and concentrate on establishing the Positive Behavior Expectations (PBEs) and the Redirect Behavior Model (RBM) within the first couple of months of the semester. It is a model that can establish behavior and content concurrently.

- *Communication:* inform students of behavior and academic expectations

- *Accountability:* create a culture of accountability shared by the teacher and students

- *Leadership:* teachers and students both have opportunities to lead students to success

- *Motivation:* innovative methods that are easily implemented to engage students

All of these components build upon one another; however, the major tenets of the CALM methods are based on a culture of developing relationships, respect, trust, and a unifying purpose of student success.

Reflection Questions

- As you begin to think about your classroom, what are your biggest concerns regarding behavior management?

- If you have been in the classroom for more than one year, what were your successes? What were your biggest challenges?

Quick Wins

This is a comprehensive system that can be implemented in the classroom or a schoolwide initiative. Part of starting small and building upon successes is finding your quick wins. Quick wins are the small-scale wins to achieve the big win. For example, if a student is resistant to working with a group, start small and build upon each win. Begin by having the student sit with the group. This is a quick win. Next time, have them take notes while they are with their group. Another quick win. Next, have the student share one idea with the group. Continue to build upon each quick win. The long-term goal would be to have the student participate fully within each cooperative learning group activity. We will be noting the quick wins as we progress through each strategy.

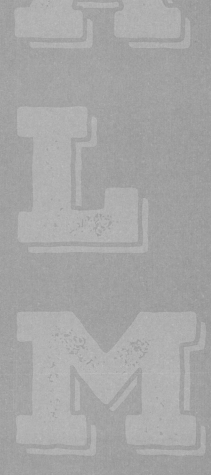

PART I

COMMUNICATION

Positive Behavior Expectations

Mrs. Smith is a ninth-grade English teacher. She loves the students, but she is finding it difficult to address disruptive behavior. She seems to write an inordinate number of referrals. Every time she asks students to stop talking, they ignore her and continue to talk, or they begin to argue with her.

The discourse on any given day in Mrs. Smith's classroom could be viewed as combative, argumentative, and at times disrespectful. For the most part, Mrs. Smith feels she gets along fine with the students; however, the students often question why they are asked to complete certain tasks and have difficulty getting along in small-group activities. Mrs. Smith feels there is a disconnect between her communication and the students talking to her and among their peers.

Mrs. Smith has no idea how to get her students to talk to her and one another with more respect. So far, her only course of action has been to tell students to stop talking. It seems that is her catch phrase. After repeating that phrase multiple times throughout a class period, her frustrations and voice volume begin to escalate while her patience diminishes. She sends the same three to five students to the office so often that eventually they are suspended; unfortunately, they miss a great deal of instruction time and quickly fall behind. This means Mrs. Smith has to spend more time reteaching and preparing other, alternative materials for those students. Mrs. Smith feels as if she is doing more work and their behavior hasn't changed. She knows there has to be a better way to address the disruptive behavior.

As we learned in the previous chapter, it is important to teach Positive Behavior Expectations (PBEs) so that students are able to understand exactly what is expected of them in order to be successful. The Redirect Behavior Model is a method that helps teach and reinforce the behavior expectations. We'll go over that in Chapter 3. It will empower the teacher to take on the role of facilitator, where the students are held accountable for their own actions according to their choices.

The goal of teaching PBEs is to establish a structured environment and a supportive culture where students are able to be successful. Rules and procedures contribute to bringing this about.

What do proactive strategies truly look like? What do they sound like? The activities in this chapter will help you and your students cocreate those PBEs. Taking that extra time to address classroom behavior is the last thing you want to deal with on top of your already busy school schedule. However, I challenge you to reflect on the amount of time you spend during your busy school day addressing repeated behavior issues and also take note of your frustration levels throughout the day. If much of that time spent on reacting to classroom disruptions can be eliminated by teaching behavioral norms, wouldn't that be time well spent?

Explicit Expectations Lead to Positive Results

I am a science teacher in an urban district. I have students perform experiments in the lab, but sometimes student disruptions made it impossible to have a successful experiment. Students would talk over my instructions and gave no indication that they listened to or understood my directions. They did not realize the importance of following lab rules. I would get frustrated and didn't know how to stop the talking and all of the disrespectful behavior.

> *I asked Dr. Lentfer to come in to help me get some control in my classroom. We devised a plan to start over and have the students define respect. We then had the students list behaviors that showed respect. We came up with simple steps for the students to follow. The Positive Behavior Expectations primarily addressed talking and respecting other people's property. We also made specific Positive Behavior Expectations for the lab. Students created posters displaying the rules and their own rationales.*
>
> *Once we defined respect and had the students come up with the steps for each expectation, I felt we developed better relationships and completed our work more successfully and more efficiently. I also felt like I was more in control of the classroom without students talking during my instructions, and it reduced the chaotic behavior during lab.*
>
> Daniel Stokes,
> science, Grades 7–12

In the Research

Student behavior is one of the leading reasons why 50% of new teachers leave urban districts within the first 5 years of being hired (McKinney, Campbell-Whately, & Kea, 2005). Teachers are leaving the profession at an alarming rate of 40% to 50% in the first 5 years (Ingersoll, Merrill, & Stuckey, 2014). Novice and pre-service teachers site the lack of preparation for addressing the high needs of the diverse population (Mitchell & Arnold, 2004). Very often, teachers encounter students who exhibit persistent disruptive behavior and unmet social and emotional needs, yet our novice teachers are entering the classroom with a lack of expertise in how to address these issues (Kyriacou, Avramidis, Hoie, Stephens, & Hultgren, 2007; Niesyn, 2009; Shook, 2009). A teacher with 3 or fewer years of experience is more likely to report student behavior as a problem in their classroom (Melnick & Meister, 2008). Teachers may encounter up to 10% of their students exhibiting behavior issues that require intervention (Forness, 2005; Neary & Eyberg, 2002).

Teachers expect students to enter the classroom with established basic school behaviors such as being able to listen during instruction, raise their hand to talk, stay on task, and follow instructions without the need for the teacher to teach those skills (Beebe-Frankenberger, Lane, Bocian, Gresham, & MacMillan, 2005; Kyriacou et al., 2007). Many teachers are unaware that they have to establish these basic social skills in the beginning of each school year.

Research has shown that using proactive approaches, such as positive encouragement, has a beneficial impact on student achievement and promotes on-task behavior (Arthur, Gordon, & Butterfield, 2003). Proactive strategies are effective classroom management strategies that prevent potential disruptive behavior for all classrooms (Niesyn, 2009).

Shift in Thinking—Teaching Behavior and Content With Gradual Release

There is a gradual release of accountability in classroom behavior. Elementary teachers will address a broad spectrum of detailed behaviors such as: how to stand in a line, walk in a line, wash your hands, blow your nose, and raise your hand, just to name a few. Elementary teachers have to be explicit in addressing the behavior expectations. You may have the students develop the rationale as to why it's important for the students to follow the expectations. But the key to success is to take the time to practice the behavior and have the students try again if they did not meet the expectation.

In middle school, as the child gradually develops, the expectations will change to meet the needs of the students. The teacher may have gentle reminders for some of the elementary behaviors, such as washing hands, walking on the right-hand side of the hallway. Students may also have to practice how to line up to go to lunch and how to get the teacher's attention, but those behaviors may be determined as more of a class-by-class situation. Middle level students still need the guidance of the teacher, yet they are beginning to distinguish appropriate and inappropriate behaviors. At this stage, the students will create the PBEs in the classroom, and the teacher will gradually release the accountability to the student. The teacher's role is to observe and guide the students to understand which behaviors may need to be addressed. For example, bullying prevention may be a specific topic for the students to address in the PBEs. The class may concentrate on addressing communication in the classroom or positive interactions or relationships in the classroom. This may look and sound different for each classroom because the students are developing the expectations. The teacher's role is to observe student interactions, and if there is any negative behavior, this may be a time the teacher has the students develop another PBE to address any negative interaction.

High school will continue the progression of focusing on positive relationships and developing communication skills. Teachers may wish to concentrate on teaching students how to have conversations with differing viewpoints, use encouraging words in a team atmosphere, accept feedback from the teacher and peers, and work with others when there are personality conflicts. These are 21st-century skills that are critical to the success of students inside and outside of the classroom.

Continue to observe behaviors. As the behaviors that may not be desirable arise, invite the students to address the behavior. For example, if the teacher finds that there are some students who may have differing viewpoints, address this with the whole class, but in a conversational tone. Discuss a time when you worked in a group in which all the team members may not have shared the same idea. How did you feel? How did you work through the challenges? Furthermore, talk through the situation with your class and develop a new PBE that addresses how to work with others when you do not share the same viewpoint.

The gradual release progresses as the teacher and students develop trust and develop their relationships. Ultimately, in order to have a team community, the students are at the center of decision making and the teacher is there to guide, observe, and follow through with the expectations.

Assumptions can get the best of us. For example, teachers often assume that students know how to raise their hands, not to talk during instruction, or how to talk cooperatively with a partner. However, it doesn't take long before you realize students may not be behaving as you envisioned. Your students need you to provide them instruction on how to be the best learners they can be. Meet them where they are. I challenge you to approach behavior as you would approach content.

Would you teach the quadratic formula by assuming they know how to plug in the numbers, implement the appropriate steps to calculate the formula, solve the problem, and know why the formula is important? No; you would introduce the material, model the appropriate steps to calculate and solve the problem, and offer a rationale as to how and why the formula is important. You would use the gradual release method by first introducing and modeling and then allowing students to practice and eventually solve independently—whether they are solving the quadratic formula or an interpersonal conflict in the classroom.

The gradual release method also works when teaching behavior. You introduce the desired behavior, teach the steps to successfully display the behavior, and offer a rationale as to why the behavior is important to the success of the student and the classroom community. Students then practice the behavior, and eventually they will be able to display the appropriate behavior independently.

Some students will be able to demonstrate the appropriate behavior with minimal practice. However, other students may need additional practice and guidance. Keep in mind that students learn content and behavior at different paces. This will allow you to remain calm when a student may need extra guidance. Teaching behavior at the beginning of the year is the best time to catch students while they are attentive and open to learning new skills. Introduce the behavior, teach the students how to display the behavior, and eventually the students may need a simple prompt regarding their behavior.

> Teaching behavior is the same as teaching content. Introduce the behavior, teach them how to display the behavior, develop steps to attain the goal, practice, and eventually be able to make good choices and become independent thinkers.

The novice teacher will have to use their time liberally while establishing PBEs. Take the time to involve students in building the culture in the classroom. Do not panic and go directly into content. You may integrate content as you are teaching your expectations.

Proactive Teaching

Creating PBEs is a part of a proactive teaching practice. What does proactive teaching mean? What does it sound like? What does it look like?

In part, being proactive is being able to identify what behaviors you want to see in the classroom and address those behaviors prior to an activity or lesson. In doing so, you are addressing potential misbehavior before it transpires.

Proactive strategies can prevent potential classroom disruptions (Lannie & McCurdy, 2007; Stormont & Reinke, 2009). A sample of proactive strategies may include discussing rules and procedures, providing effective praise, establishing classroom procedures, defining on-task behavior, addressing social skills, and explaining teacher expectations (Barton-Arwood, Morrow, Lane, & Jolivette, 2005; Lannie & McCurdy, 2007; Shook, 2009; Stormont & Reinke, 2009). We will work on these strategies together in the activities later in this chapter.

To successfully implement proactive strategies, developing respect within your classroom is imperative. Respect is often the most common value teachers and students name when describing what they need from each other. Don't assume that your students know how to be respectful in the classroom. Most classrooms consist of students from diverse backgrounds where definitions of respect vary from person to person, culture to culture. As a classroom community, discuss the significance of respect and together work toward definitions of what acting respectful looks like on a day-to-day basis. Be prepared to proactively teach students how to do everything from sharpening their pencils (elementary) to interacting cooperatively in small work groups (high school).

So often, we assume our students and peers share our definitions of certain values. What we think is evident may not be as clear or have the same meaning for others. Many different factors play a part in this. Classroom communities are comprised of different cultures, different primary languages, different family expectations, as well as other differences that affect how we define values.

Early in my career it became very clear to me that people's idea of respect can vary greatly from one person to the next. A fifth-grade student was getting up to sharpen his pencil several times while another student was presenting in front of the whole class. I asked the student not to sharpen his pencil during the presentation and said he would be able to sharpen his pencil when the presentation was over. Simple request, right? He instantly told me that I was disrespectful and not to talk to him like that. At first, I felt terrible for making someone feel disrespected. But as I began to reflect, I realized that what I had asked of him was a reasonable request. If he really did think my request was disrespectful maybe we, as a class, needed to have a clearer definition of respect. I had the students define the word *respect*. Their answers were as varied as snowflakes in a blizzard. They were similar in that they agreed it was how to treat people. All of their definitions were absolutely correct, and we embraced all of their ideas. As a class we decided to simplify the definition to: *Be kind; don't be mean to each other.*

While the definition of respect can vary from person to person, class to class, the important idea is to focus on how to show respect. Positive Behavior Expectations outline how to show respect. It is a method whereby the classroom community identifies/supports the actual actions that people take when interacting with one another and support this effort with a rationale.

Proactive Versus Reactive

Have you heard yourself repeating these short phrases in your classroom? *Sit down. Stop talking. Be quiet. Turn around. Keep your hands to yourself. One at a time. Pay attention.* These short phrases are referred to as reactive responses. While reactive responses may prompt the student to stop immediately, they are a short-term solution to a long-term behavior dilemma. Reactive strategies can ignite and escalate behavior issues (Barton-Arwood, Morrow, Lane, & Jolivette, 2005; Mitchell & Arnold, 2004). Teachers that predominantly rely on reactive methods also show a higher rate of stress and student on-task behavior decreases (Clunies-Ross, Little, & Kienhuis, 2008). The lack of knowledge and a belief in proactive strategies is often cited as the cause of using a reactive method (Peters, 2012; Smart & Brent, 2010).

Inside or outside of the classroom, we have all resorted to reactive behavior requests that we repeat over and over. Reactive responses elicit an immediate reaction, but the inappropriate behavior can reoccur quite quickly. In fact, in my experience, it may be as short as 2 minutes between redirections. Reactive responses may have a negative effect or no effect at all, depending upon the circumstances. A considerable amount of research has suggested reactive teacher interactions and punitive reprimands increase student disruptions (Beaman & Wheldall, 2000; Stormont, Smith, & Lewis, 2007; Thomas, Becker, & Armstrong, 1968).

Reactive strategies can be repeated requests that intensify disruptive behavior (Barton-Arwood et al., 2005; Mitchell & Arnold, 2004). When a teacher spends too much time addressing behavior after the disruption it decreases the amount of instructional time for all the students in the class (Fernley, 2011). With all of the daily educational demands placed upon teachers and students, actual instructional time is paramount for student achievement. Furthermore, after you have addressed the inappropriate behavior multiple times using reactive responses, then there is a need to invoke consequences. Many times, educators will have the student stay in before or after school or during lunch, which can take time away from preparing lessons, extracurricular activities, and family time.

In addition to expending time and energy, a teacher's level of frustration intensifies when the redirection doesn't seem to have a positive impact on the student or the learning environment.

Some questions you may ask yourself when using reactive responses are: What are the students learning when I make reactive statements? Am I taking the time to explicitly communicate what students need to do (or not do) to be successful? Are they learning how to respect one another? Are they learning how to respect themselves?

> If you want students to behave respectfully, you have to proactively teach them how to behave respectfully rather than reacting when they are disrespectful.

The traditional approach to reacting to poor behavior can be punitive and exclusionary, which fails to prevent disruptive behavior and fosters a

I didn't think about the reactive approach. In fact, this is what I remember how some of my teachers used to talk to us. I knew that being proactive is important, but I didn't know how. When Dr. Lentfer introduced her proactive strategies a lightbulb went off. This was a different approach, but one students were receptive to. I didn't realize how being specific regarding exactly what I needed from the students would help them. I thought that they would see me as too picky, but the students didn't even question any of my strategies.

Maria Reyes-Vazquez
English, Grades 7–12

negative culture in the classroom. In contrast, implementing positive, proactive measures to instruct students regarding desired behavior may eradicate problems before they occur. Beginning with a positive outlook will lead to a constructive, encouraging, student-centered classroom. The bottom line is, if you want students to behave respectfully, you have to proactively teach them how to behave respectfully rather than reacting when they are disrespectful.

Time to Teach

I have found that the first 2 weeks of school is the time when students are most attentive. This is the best time to teach students PBEs, thereby establishing a positive classroom culture from Day One. Whether students want to admit it or not, they are actually excited to be back in school and are more open to learning new material.

Here is where the majority of teachers ask, "What about content?" It turns out that teaching content alongside Positive Behavior Expectations is crucial to the successful adoption of those expectations. The key concept to note is that during the first 2 weeks, the emphasis of teaching will be 95% on teaching behavior expectations and 5% on content. By taking the first 2 weeks to focus primarily on teaching PBEs, you will set the tone for how well your classroom will progress for the remainder of the school year. For the first several weeks they will be fairly well behaved. Catch the students being good. By positively reinforcing their good behavior and making explicit connections between their good behavior and the behavior expectations under discussion, you will create a positive classroom culture where cooperative norms are established that will replicate themselves throughout the year. A well-organized and managed classroom not only has a positive influence on student interactions, it also positively influences student achievement (Marzano, Marzano, & Pickering, 2003). The PBEs will set the tone for how well your classroom will progress.

> By taking the first 2 weeks to focus primarily on teaching Positive Behavior Expectations, you will set the tone for how well your classroom will progress for the remainder of the school year.

Gradually, time spent on teaching behavior expectations will decrease and time teaching content will increase. Even though I have emphasized reserving the first 2 weeks of school, every classroom is different. Some teachers may have to reserve the first month to establish PBEs.

Beginning the CALM Classroom Process

My teaching motto was based on seven simple words: "Make Good Choices. Do the Right Thing." If you present students with all of the choices, and indicate both positive and negative outcomes, they will be well-informed and will be in control of their own decision making. But they also have to be able to accept the consequences of the outcome based on their choices.

The motto worked in conjunction with the idea of defining respect. The PBEs defined respect, and the motto prompted the students to remember to make good choices and do the right thing. Technology changes, leadership changes, but respect is one skill that will propel you further professionally and personally. People will always be expected to make good choices and do the right thing. So how do we begin this process?

Beginning the CALM Classroom Process

1. Visualize and describe your ideal classroom.

2. Identify the five essential Positive Behavior Expectations (PBEs).

(Continued)

(Continued)

3. Identify 3–5 steps to successfully achieve each PBE.

4. Identify a rationale for each PBE.

5. Create a poster for each of the five PBEs.

6. Reinforce the PBEs.

ACTIVITY #1

Visualize and describe your ideal classroom

Prior to school beginning, take a moment to visualize the ideal classroom and make it as perfect as possible. Note every detail in order to create a classroom that will promote a safe, productive learning environment. Visualize different situations that may occur in the classroom and how you would react if they do. What does your classroom look like during the first month? What does it look like halfway through the year? Fast-forward and envision how your classroom will look at the end of the year.

Why is this important? You have to begin with a vision before you are able to execute the plan. Visualize the outcome, create goals, execute a plan, and expect amazing results. It will provide the pathway. This is the first step in having a CALM Classroom.

I thought at first this was crazy to visualize what my ideal classroom would look like. Dr. Lentfer even had us visualize what it would sound and smell like. I thought that this would never work. She continued to refer to this activity as we were developing our classroom management plan. I didn't think any of these things mattered. But when I got into the classroom, I realized these key details made a difference in the organization and student behavior. I have since continued to visualize. In fact, it has helped me to gain confidence as a teacher because I will visualize what and how I teach on a daily basis.

Marisol Fernandez,
science, Grades 7–12

Let's begin the CALM Management process. Write down everything you envisioned, and be as detailed as possible. Here are some ideas to consider while visualizing:

Culture	What is the feel of the classroom? —warm, inviting, inclusive, valued
	What is the first impression?
	Would a parent or student be inspired to come back to your room?
Wall art	Can you see encouraging messages, inclusive art, student art, or artifacts that tell your story?
Literacy	Do you have multicultural literature, picture books, all genres available?
	How are they displayed?
	Is there a reading area that is comfortable?
Sound	Is there music that represents all cultures?
	Can you hear positive conversations?
Voice	Are voice levels appropriate?
	Are students engaging in productive discourse?
	Are students generating appropriate voice inflections?
Noise	What is the noise level?
	Is there a low hum of conversation or a cacophony of shouts and jabs?
	Is there laughter?
	Is there silence?
Talking	Who is doing most of the talking—teacher or students?
	Do students raise their hands?
	Do students wait to be called upon?
	Are the conversations on-topic?
Smell	Does it smell good?
	Are there air fresheners?
	Do you have a window open?

(Continued)

(Continued)

Teacher	Is the teacher doing all the work?
	Is the teacher off to the side facilitating?
	Is there a shared workload between the students and teacher?
Students	Are students on-task, productive, and supportive of one another?
	Where are your students from? What do you know of their personalities and personal cultures? What are their backgrounds?
Seating arrangement	Are students sitting in rows or pods of desks?
	Are students able to walk easily between each desk or pod?
	Can they move into rows or groups easily?
Technology	Is technology integrated into the curriculum?
	Are students using their devices appropriately?
	Is it a paperless classroom?
	Are you skyping with students from other countries?
	Are students recording themselves teaching?
	Is technology used to substitute, augment, modify, or redefine the curriculum?
Movement	Are students keeping their hands and feet to themselves while walking?
	Are they moving at the appropriate time?
	Are they talking while they are moving, or are they quiet?
Individual work	Are students in their seats quietly working?
	Is the teacher off to the side facilitating?
Partner work	Are students talking and working together?
	Are they on-task?
	Is the teacher to the side facilitating?
Group work	Are students collaborating in a supportive manner?
	Are all students engaged?
	Is the teacher to the side facilitating?

Presenting	Are students presenting their findings?
	Are students quiet while others are presenting?
	Do they ask relevant questions after each presentation?

Keep these ideas in mind as you begin to develop your CALM Management plan. All of the details listed should parallel your expectations for your classroom and students. This vision will define your ideal classroom and what you represent.

ACTIVITY #2

Task Analysis:

Identify the five foundational Positive Behavior Expectations

Keep in mind that the expectations will define what respect will look and sound like in the classroom. Begin with five PBEs. The five should be general and nonspecific to content. Normally, they address an element of talking and working—independently, or potentially with other students (partner or small-group). Talking tends to be the most prevalent disruption teachers encounter throughout their day. These five expectations will serve as a starting point. As the semester progresses, you will add more as the behaviors emerge for each class.

Have students develop the five foundational PBEs and rationales. This empowers them to have a voice in what the behaviors are and how they will look and sound in the classroom.

The role of the teacher is to prompt students with questions as to how their ideas may impact the class community. Help them with their wording with the steps—less is more. Which steps are necessary? And why is the behavior important?

1. *Brainstorm.* Have students brainstorm particular behaviors that enable them to interact with one another respectfully in the classroom.

2. *Construct steps.* Together, students identify 3–5 simple steps to successfully achieve each behavior expectation.

3. *Construct rationale*. Together, students identify rationales for each of the five foundational PBEs.

Begin by making a three-column chart that will help to identify the five essential PBEs that define respect.

Identifying Five Essential Positive Behavior Expectations			
Five Behaviors That Define RESPECT	**Classroom Behavior You Would Like to See**	**What Does the Behavior Look Like?**	**What Does the Behavior Sound Like?**
Behavior #1	Students raising their hands	Students asking and answering questions the teacher poses	One person speaking while others listening. No talking
Behavior #2	Students working independently	Working and staying on-task	No talking
Behavior #3	Students listening to one another	One person talking and other students not talking, but giving eye contact to the speaker and nodding their head, indicating they are listening	One person talking and other students not talking
Behavior #4	Students entering the classroom and beginning their work	Students walking in a calm manner with their materials and beginning working. Keeping their hands and feet to themselves	Students talking in a low volume as they begin their work
Behavior #5	Students listening and following the directions the teacher presents and the directions for assignments	Students reading or listening to the directions and beginning the task	Students asking clarifying questions, if needed, by raising their hands

In the first column, list five behaviors you would like to see displayed on a consistent basis in your classroom. In the second column, list what the behaviors in the first column look like. In the third column, list what the behaviors in the first column sound like. Be as specific as possible.

Analyze the columns and begin to identify the five essential PBEs that define respect. In particular, look at each row and pick out a word that summarizes the behavior. For example, in behavior #1 in row one, the behavior addresses students raising their hands and answering or asking questions the teacher poses. You could identify the behavior as Raising Your Hand to Talk in Class, or shorten it to Raise Your Hand.

> Remember, you are defining respect; try not to use the word *respect* in the definition.

To define respect, it will encompass a wide variety of behaviors. By not having the word *respect* in the definition it will force you to be specific in the expected behavior. For example, you may have stated that you want students to speak respectfully. How might you teach students to speak respectfully? Is it in their tone? Is it in the words they choose? What does that sound and look like? Maybe you want students to raise their hand before they speak so it ensures all student voices may be heard.

I thought this task seemed tedious. What student doesn't know how to raise their hand? But when I went into the classroom it quickly became apparent the nonstop talking during class was out of control. I am going to do the task analysis method before I get my classroom. But I suspect most of my expectations are going to be centered around talking.

Garrin Leahy,
middle school, math

ACTIVITY #3

Identify 3–5 steps to successfully achieve each Positive Behavior Expectation

As a class you have agreed upon and identified the five foundational PBEs. Now let's create steps for students to follow to successfully achieve the behavior expectation. The steps should be sequential, simple, and easy to follow. Limit the steps to 3–5 to keep it easy to remember and attainable. For example:

Raise Your Hand

- Quietly raise your hand.

- Patiently wait for the teacher's acknowledgment before speaking.

- Calmly state your answer or ask your question.

> Look closely at the "Looks like" and "Sounds like" columns. These often provide some ideas to identify the steps for students to follow.

Five Behaviors That Define RESPECT	Classroom Behaviors You Would Like to See
Behavior #1	Raising Your Hand
Step 1	Quietly raise your hand
Step 2	Patiently wait for the teacher's acknowledgment before speaking
Step 3	Calmly state your answer or ask your question
Step 4	
Step 5	
Behavior #2	Maintain Working on an Assignment
Step 1	Begin the assignment

Five Behaviors That Define RESPECT	Classroom Behaviors You Would Like to See
Step 2	Ignore surrounding disruptions
Step 3	Concentrate your full effort on completing the assignment
Step 4	
Step 5	
Behavior #3	Listening to Others
Step 1	Keep your eyes on the person speaking
Step 2	Continue to maintain voice level 0
Step 3	Center attention on speaker
Step 4	Wait until they have finished before asking a question or making a comment
Step 5	Thank them for their time
Behavior #4	Entering the Classroom
Step 1	Walk with your hands or feet to self
Step 2	Keep low voice tone
Step 3	Go directly to your seat
Step 4	Begin the bellwork or classroom starter
Step 5	
Behavior #5	Following Directions
Step 1	Listen to directions
Step 2	Read directions
Step 3	Ask clarifying questions
Step 4	Begin the assignment
Step 5	

Invite students to identify the behaviors and construct the steps.
Employ question prompts that will lead students to identifying your five

foundational behaviors. Or you may post the five foundational behaviors and have students create the steps and rationale for each. By allowing students to be a part of the process, it will increase their "buy-in" to the PBEs.

Suggestions for Elementary Students

- Have the 3–5 steps completed and posted for students to view.

- Have students draw pictures to represent the steps and post.

- Have students record themselves following the steps and post or send to parents.

Suggestions for Middle School/High School Students

- Have students create the 3–5 easy steps to follow.

ACTIVITY #4

Identify a rationale for each Positive Behavior Expectation

Identifying Five Foundational Positive Behavior Expectations				
Five Behaviors That Define RESPECT	**Classroom Behavior You Would Like to See**	**What Does the Behavior Look Like?**	**What Does the Behavior Sound Like?**	**Rationale**
Behavior #1	Raising Your Hand	Students asking and answering questions the teacher poses	One person speaking while others listening. No talking	Exercising this behavior will help strengthen your self-control and improve your ability to communicate in a calm manner.
Step 1	Quietly raise your hand			
Step 2	Patiently wait for teacher's acknowledgment before speaking			
Step 3	Calmly state your answer or ask your question			
Step 4				
Step 5				

Identifying Five Foundational Positive Behavior Expectations				
Five Behaviors That Define RESPECT	Classroom Behavior You Would Like to See	What Does the Behavior Look Like?	What Does the Behavior Sound Like?	Rationale
Behavior #2	Maintain Working on an Assignment	Working and staying on-task	No talking	It's important to be able to develop a strong work ethic so you are able to complete an assignment with great efficiency.
Step 1	Begin the assignment			
Step 2	Ignore surrounding disruptions			
Step 3	Concentrate your full effort on completing the assignment			
Step 4				
Step 5				
Behavior #3	Listening to Others	One person talking and other students not talking, but giving eye contact to the speaker and nodding their head, indicating they are listening	One person talking and other students not talking	It communicates that you value other people's thoughts and opinions.
Step 1	Keep your eyes on the person speaking			
Step 2	Maintain voice level 0			
Step 3	Center attention on speaker			

(Continued)

(Continued)

Identifying Five Foundational Positive Behavior Expectations				
Five Behaviors That Define RESPECT	Classroom Behavior You Would Like to See	What Does the Behavior Look Like?	What Does the Behavior Sound Like?	Rationale
Step 4	Wait until they have finished before asking a question or making a comment			
Step 5	Thank them for their time			
Behavior #4	Entering the Classroom	Students walking in a calm manner with their materials and beginning working. They keep their hands and feet to themselves	Students talking in a low volume as they begin their work	By entering the classroom with purpose they will begin the day or class on a positive note. It will keep you safe and prepared to begin the classwork.
Step 1	Walk with your hands and feet to self			
Step 2	Low voice tone			
Step 3	Go directly to your seat			
Step 4	Begin the bellwork or classroom starter			
Step 5				
Behavior #5	Following Directions	Students reading or listening to the directions and beginning the task	Students asking clarifying questions, if needed, by raising their hands	Allows students to efficiently complete work without disrupting classmates.
Step 1	Listen to directions			

Identifying Five Foundational Positive Behavior Expectations				
Five Behaviors That Define RESPECT	Classroom Behavior You Would Like to See	What Does the Behavior Look Like?	What Does the Behavior Sound Like?	Rationale
Step 2	Read the directions			
Step 3	Ask clarifying questions			
Step 4	Begin the assignment			
Step 5				

Many times teachers find that what seems like a simple request for students to follow often prompts them to ask, "Why?" Providing a rationale gives the expectation a purpose, which if communicated correctly can emphasize that the teacher values, respects, and empathizes with the student. Have the students develop the rationale. This will further the idea of empowering the student with their voice and sharing their thoughts and ideas.

Having the students participate in creating the steps just helps with the students to buy-in to the classroom culture.

Garrin Leahy,
middle school, math

List the rationale after the steps for each PBE. Keep in mind that the listed rationale is a starting point; there can be many reasons why it is important to properly get the teacher's attention. For example, it is important because . . . everyone can hear everyone's ideas, it lessens the distractions during instruction and discussion, and someone may be too shy to answer or ask a question, so your ideas may address their question. The list is endless, but to have a general rationale that everyone can see and follow is a good starting point.

Suggestions for Elementary School

- Have students record themselves stating the PBE; state the steps and rationale. Post, or have the recording available for parents and/or during parent conferences.

- Practice the expected behaviors together as a class until they display the expectation to perfection.

- Follow through and have the students redo any behavior that did not meet your standards—be firm in your follow-through and expectations.

Suggestions for Middle School

- Have students create their own rationale. Post the rationales.

- Practice until perfect.

- Follow through and have the student redo the expectation until it is to your standard—be firm in your follow-through and expectations.

- Concentrate on the social skills that may deter bullying—i.e., how to show empathy, how to apologize, how to advocate for self, how to advocate for others, take responsibility for their actions, self-reflect on their actions, be aware when they feel like they are going to bully.

- Concentrate on communicating their ideas with respect and support for all students.

- Consider addressing technology use—cell phones, social media.

Suggestions for High School

- Have students create their own rationale. Post the rationales.

- Practice the expectation.

- Follow through and have the student redo the expectation until it is to your standard—be firm in your follow-through and expectations.

- Concentrate on the social skills that may deter bullying—i.e., how to show empathy, how to apologize, how to advocate for self, how to advocate for others, take responsibility for their actions, self-reflect on their actions, be aware when they feel like they are going to bully.

- Concentrate on communicating their ideas with respect and support for all students.

- Consider addressing technology use—cell phones, social media.

ACTIVITY #5

Students create a poster for each Positive Behavior Expectation they identified

Students create a poster for each behavior and hang the posters in the classroom as a visual resource. Encourage students to use pictures to communicate their ideas.

> I was a pre-service teacher facing one of my first practicum experiences. I had Dr. Lentfer for my instructor and she taught us about the Positive Behavior Expectations, Redirect Behavior Model, and Voice Movement Task. I was placed in a high school physics class. I met my mentor teacher in the practicum and through my observation I noted that the class was very talkative during instruction and were on their phones as well. I told my mentor teacher that I had been learning some classroom management techniques, and asked if he'd be willing for me to try a few things. His eyes lit up and he said I could take a full class period to go over classroom management strategies.
>
> The lesson consisted of coming up with four behaviors we could agree upon as a class. I engaged the students in the process and we came up with: Raising Your Hand, No Cell Phones During Instruction, No Talking During Instruction, and Following Directions. The class agreed upon these four and developed the steps and rationale. I took over this classroom a few months into the semester. At first, the students were reluctant because they hadn't been asked their opinion or invited to be a part of the class expectations with
>
> *(Continued)*

(Continued)

the mentor teacher. But once we started the process the students began to take charge. They really enjoyed role-playing the correct and incorrect ways to show the five behaviors. Together, my mentor teacher and I followed through with the expectations, and it provided a more calm and productive learning environment. In fact, I noticed some of the students began to sit up more and ask more questions. This was a physics class, so some of the students may have been hesitant to participate because of the difficulty of the material, but once we established the Positive Behavior Expectations and involved the students, they had a more collaborative feel toward one another.

Chris Jackson,
science, Grades 7–12

Begin with five Positive Behavior Expectations. You will add more as you may note behaviors that need to be addressed. Begin small and build. I found the five I listed began the semester and the class to a good start.

Here are some common PBEs with which you may wish to start (or may suggest for your students to consider):

1. **Raise Your Hand**
   - Quietly raise your hand.
   - Patiently wait for the teacher's acknowledgment before speaking.
   - Calmly state your answer or ask your question.

Rationale: Provides an opportunity for all students to share opinions, ideas, and questions so that everyone can learn from one another.

2. **Maintain Working on an Assignment**
   - Begin the assignment.

- Ignore surrounding disruptions.
- Concentrate your full effort on completing the assignment.

Rationale: It's important to be able to develop a strong work ethic so you are able to complete an assignment with great efficiency.

3. **Listen to Others**
   - Keep your eyes on the person speaking.
   - Maintain voice level 0.
   - Center attention on the speaker.
   - Wait until they have finished before asking a question or making a comment.
   - Thank them for their time.

Rationale: It communicates that you value other people's thoughts and opinions.

4. **Enter the Classroom**
   - Walk with your hands and feet to self.
   - Keep low voice volume.
   - Go directly to your seat.
   - Begin the bellwork or classroom starter.

Rationale: By entering the classroom with purpose they will begin the day or class on a positive note. It will keep you safe and prepared to begin the classwork.

5. **Follow Directions**
   - Listen to directions.
   - Read directions.
   - Ask clarifying questions.
   - Begin the assignment.

Rationale: Allows students to efficiently complete work without disrupting classmates.

I didn't think the students would like me to introduce more rules for them to follow. But when I introduced the Positive Behavior Expectation of How to Raise Your Hand, the students didn't seem to mind. I had them practice and I felt better because now I told them what I expected and had a poster for them to refer to as well. I assumed they knew exactly how to raise their hand, but if I didn't let them know that is what I expected, they would continue to talk whenever they felt like it.

Sarah Bohrer,
middle level, language arts

6. **No Talking During Instruction**
   - Maintain voice level 0.
   - Raise your hand to make comments or ask questions at appropriate moments.
   - Follow any instructions.
   - Take notes when appropriate.
   - Focus your attention on the material presented.

Rationale: Staying focused and quiet will allow you to begin to comprehend the material and not to fall behind in the course work.

7. **Conversation One-to-One**
   - Listen to the person speaking.
   - Wait until they have finished.
   - Communicate your idea or question with positive word choices.
   - Thank them for listening.

Rationale: People will want to talk to you more because conversing respectfully shows you value what others have to say.

8. **Class Conversation**
   - Listen to all comments.
   - Consider all aspects of the topic.
   - Wait calmly to communicate your ideas and questions.
   - Communicate on-topic ideas and questions.
   - Be sensitive of others.
   - Thank people for their ideas and questions.

Rationale: Listening to everyone's opinions and ideas and considering everyone's side of the story will help you to understand and value all perspectives.

9. **Independent Work**

- Think about what you need to complete.

- Begin the assignment.

- Ignore all distractions.

- Submit the assignment appropriately.

Rationale: It is important to process and complete work on your own to develop critical thinking skills.

10. **Small-Group Interactions**

- Listen to everyone's ideas.

- Wait until it is your turn to speak.

- Offer your ideas/questions.

- Share materials/ideas/questions equally.

- Thank people for sharing their ideas/ questions/materials.

I thought the practice would be a waste of time, but the kids loved acting out the right and the wrong way to perform the expectations. We had fun!

Sarah Bohrer,
middle level, language arts

Rationale: Sharing ideas/questions/materials will allow everyone to feel valued and a part of the team.

Bullying

The CALM method is a wonderful program to use when dealing with bullying. It is setting the expectation and being able to use the Redirect Behavior Model (RBM) in a conversational style to help guide the conversation and self-reflection with the bullying situation. The Positive Behavior Expectations assist the student and teacher to engage in meaningful dialogue focusing on self-reflection and how to be more aware of actions and emotions. It allows the bully to explore why they bully. It places the responsibility on the bully to understand why they do it and make the necessary adjustments accordingly. When a teacher helps the student understand why they bully, it places the responsibility back on the student.

I understand this may take time, but having the tools or a system in place to begin the dialogue is of great value. The guidance counselor or administrator may go beyond these conversations, but this technique is useful for a guided conversation at the student's level as well. Helping the student to understand or become aware of why they are displaying this behavior is a step in healing both the bully and the bullied.

Here are some student examples from middle school:

How to Show Empathy

- Listen to the person and/or observe the situation.

- Think of how the person is feeling.

- Think of a time you may have felt the same way.

- If you can't think of a time you may have felt the same way, begin the conversation: "I know that you are hurting right now. I'm sorry. I know when I feel hurt I want someone to listen to me." Then listen.

- Relay your story by starting with, "I understand how you may feel; I was in a similar situation." Then tell your story.

- Continue to listen and offer more stories.

- End the conversation by offering to listen any time they need someone.

Rationale: Empathy helps someone to feel better when they are hurt. It shows that you understand their pain and you care about them as a person.

How to Apologize

- Calm voice—restate the situation.

- Indicate you are sorry for [identify the area of challenge].

- State why the situation may have happened.

- State you will try to make sure it won't happen again.

- Thank them for listening.

Rationale: It is important to admit when you are wrong. This will help you to do better in the future and for the other person to feel better as well.

How to Advocate for Self

- Decide what you want or need from the situation.

- Assert yourself clearly—stay calm, stand tall.

- Express exactly what you need, in a calm tone.

- Believe in yourself and know that you have the right to advocate for yourself.

- Gather support by letting an adult know about your situation.

Rationale: It is important to be able to stand up for yourself, to let people know that you care about yourself and that you matter. It does not allow you to be isolated.

How to Advocate for Others

- Let the student know you are there for them.

- Listen to the victim.

- Let them know that you are going to tell an adult.

- Let them know it's their right to feel safe and the adult will help them.

- Let them know you are there for them any time.

- If you hear or see any dangerous situation, let an adult know about it.

Rationale: Victims have to know that there is someone there for them. Be brave and stand up for students. It's everyone's right to feel safe.

How to Take Responsibility for My Actions

- Reflect on what I was thinking before I bullied someone.

- Reflect on why I wanted to bully.

- Identify the reason: jealousy, anger, feelings of inadequacy?

- Next time I experience these feelings of anger, stop and ask myself why I am angry.

- Walk away from the situation and take time to cool down.

- Continue to be aware of my feelings, and try to be kind.

Rationale: It is important to be kind to yourself as well as others. When you are mean to people, it lets us know that you actually don't feel good about yourself.

How to Self-Reflect on My Actions

- Take a moment to think about the situation.

- Think about what I said or did in the situation.

- Think about how that may have impacted the other person/people.

- Think about how I felt about myself at the time.

- Let the person know what my thoughts and actions were in the situation.

- Apologize for my actions and try better next time.

Rationale: Rarely does someone have the total fault or blame for a situation. Everyone plays a part. It is important for you to understand your responsibility in a situation so everyone can move on.

How to Be Aware When I Feel I'm Going to Bully

- Be aware of negative feelings: anger, jealousy, etc.

- Be aware of my reactions when someone is around who I normally would pick on.

- Ask, "Why do I feel this way, what is this person doing that bothers me?"

- Search for why or what that person does that strikes negative feelings in me.

- Know that often those feelings are a threat to me because that's how I feel about myself.

Rationale: It's important to understand that it isn't always about the other person; it's usually how the bully feels about themselves. Figure out what bugs you about that person and self-reflect if that is something that may threaten you or that you may not feel good about yourself.

Suggestions for Elementary Students

Have the students use sentence starters. For example, the teacher may begin the following sentence starters:

- "I feel angry when . . . [student response]. . . ."

- "It's not nice when someone . . . [student response] . . . because . . . [student response]."

Adjust the sentence starter to fit the needs of the situation. This is how you begin to teach empathy. This activity can be whole-group, students could write their response, it could be a choral response with the teacher writing on board, or it could be a whole-group discussion. The idea is to begin the process of feeling empathy and showing how student responses influence our behaviors.

I began to teach a student who was struggling with bullying one of his classmates. I had him come in to talk about the situation. I started to teach him how to empathize, but we then started to talk about why this person made him mad. We started to realize the triggers, and he started to meet with a counselor. I felt confident in starting that conversation and not focusing on the bullying situation, but rather how the student truly felt about themselves.

Daniel Stokes,
science, Grades 7–12

ACTIVITY #6

Reinforce the Positive Behavior Expectations

1. *Check for Understanding*

Just as you would when teaching content, make checking for understanding a standard procedure when teaching PBEs. When you check for understanding, you are checking for comprehension and the student's ability to internalize the expectations. Do not assume that because you read the steps for each behavior expectation and discussed them that students have comprehended and internalized them. They will be able to demonstrate the PBE with proficiency.

2. *Ask Students to Draw an Example of What a Particular Positive Behavior Expectation Looks Like or Sounds Like*

Have students draw their own example of what the behavior expectation may look or sound like. Having the student represent their interpretation of the expectations will enhance their comprehension as well as increase the chance the student will follow the expectation. Post the drawings or have them available in a binder for future reference. This can be a great conversation starter if a student is having difficulty displaying the appropriate behavior.

3. *Role-Play: Model It, Expect It, and It Will Happen*

Have students role-play the correct and incorrect way to achieve a particular behavior expectation.

Example: Enter the Classroom Like a Student Ready to Learn

1. *After all of the students are seated, ask a volunteer to exit the classroom and then reenter, demonstrating how to enter the classroom like a student ready to learn.*

2. *Ask students:*
   - *What did [Student A] do well?*
   - *How do you know [Student A] entered the classroom correctly?*
   - *How might [Student A] improve their entry into the classroom?*

- *Why is it important to enter the classroom displaying the positive behaviors?*

3. *Ask for a second volunteer to demonstrate how* not *to enter the classroom.*
   - *What did [Student B] do incorrectly?*
   - *How do you know [Student B] entered the classroom incorrectly?*
   - *How might [Student B] improve their entry into the classroom?*
   - *What are the consequences of entering the classroom incorrectly?*

4. *Ask students to identify the correct steps to entering the classroom.*
   - *Why is it so important to follow the steps for entering the classroom?*

5. *Ask students to identify the rationale.*
   - *Why is it important to follow these steps or display this behavior?*
   - *How will this impact their learning environment?*
   - *How will this impact developing their team community environment?*

Teaching a PBE should only take 5 minutes of class time. If it takes longer than 5 minutes to address a behavior, you may run the risk of losing students' attention.

Having the students role-play is important because it is an active demonstration for interpreting students' knowledge for behavior expectations. It takes time, but if you concentrate on 2–3 behaviors each day, you will easily be able to address up to 30 behaviors within the first month. Reminders specifically addressing behavior prior to a lesson or activity are effective in reducing off-task behaviors (Smith, Lewis, & Stormont, 2011).

> Teaching a Positive Behavior Expectation should only take 5 minutes of class time. If it takes longer than 5 minutes to address a behavior, you may run the risk of losing students' attention.

4. *Practice Until Perfect*

It is important for teachers to have students practice a behavior until it is perfect. Yes, I did say "perfect." Requiring students to perfect PBEs communicates clearly the teacher's expectations but also instills in them a sense of pride and ownership for their positive behavior.

Practice until perfect is primarily directed toward whole- or small-group interactions. For example, if students did not properly follow the steps for entering the classroom, have the students stand up, line up outside of the classroom, and reenter the classroom. If there is even one infraction, start the process over without indicating which step they did not follow. I initially may prompt the students to self-identify their mistakes, but after practicing many times, the students will begin to be aware of the steps for entering and begin to self-correct their mistakes. Remember, if you expect it, the students will rise to the occasion.

Practice until perfect is used with lining up to go to lunch, cleaning up after an activity, moving during stations, and any other small- or large-group situations.

5. *Assign a Writing Activity*

As a lesson starter, have students write the steps and rationale for a particular PBE. You may also have students write the steps and rationale for a particular PBE as an exit slip.

Special Situations

Here are some special situations to consider when thinking about how to pre-teach behaviors for the following:

- Technology
  - Computer Cart
    - How to put away (one person, rows)
    - Check to make sure computers are plugged in

- ○ Computers/iPads/Any Technology
  - How to close the lids
  - How to type—don't slam the keys or rearrange keys on keyboard
  - How to take out and put away
  - How to hold or handle
- Field trip
  - ○ Bus Ride
    - Trash in trash can—not out the window
    - Hands and all body parts stay in bus—don't hang your head out the window
    - No tagging—anywhere
    - Thank the bus driver
  - ○ Clothing
    - Determine if you need a jacket
    - Is it school-appropriate?
  - ○ Walking With Group
    - Walk with purpose
    - Stay with group—no lagging behind
  - ○ Speaker
    - Give eye contact
    - Listen without talking
    - Raise hand for questions/comments
    - Ask relevant, appropriate questions—give examples
    - Sit up when they are talking
    - Act interested
    - Thank them for their time
  - ○ Restrooms
    - Wash your hands
    - Don't flood the toilets
    - No tagging

- Guest Speaker
  - Sit up at your desk
  - Take notes if appropriate
  - Raise your hand to ask a question
  - Ask relevant questions
  - Thank them for their time

- School Assembly
  - Walk as a group to the auditorium
  - Walk on the right-hand side of hall/stairwell
  - No pushing or shoving
  - Sit as a group
  - No talking/yelling or throwing things during speaker's talk
  - Wait until your teacher dismisses you

- How to Act When There Is a Substitute
  - Employ the daily routines
  - Ask if the substitute needs any assistance (when appropriate)
  - Do as the substitute asks you to do
  - If the substitute has trouble with expectations or finding items, offer to help
  - Do not leave the room until dismissed
  - Thank them for coming to your classroom
  - Remember: I always find out everything that went on ☺

Suggestions for Elementary School

- Have the PBE identified with the steps and rationale completed for the students.
- Use a series of questions to prompt students to understand what the PBE may be and why it's important.

- Use the PBEs to support classroom procedures—i.e., address the how and when: sharpen pencil, use a Kleenex, classroom materials—crayons, construction paper, etc.

- Have students draw pictures representing the behavior.

- Practice each behavior and have them do it over until they demonstrate it perfectly.

Suggestions for Middle School

- Have students identify the PBEs, the steps, and the rationale.

- Concentrate on procedures—walking down the hallway and stairwell.

Suggestions for High School

- Concentrate on communicating and showing respect.

- Consider what an engaged student may look and sound like.

- Do not assume the students know what you expect.

- Be specific.

- Take time to practice.

- Follow through—have the students redo the behavior until they are proficient.

Summary

Take the time to teach how to respect one another, and involve students in the conversation. Be specific in your expectations. And do not assume your students know what constitutes school-appropriate behavior. They may know they need to raise their hand, but they will test your limits until you explicitly state your expectations. Get the students involved in the process and follow through with the expectations.

Reflection Questions

- Was there a time when you assumed students knew what you expected and you found yourself reacting to the behavior?

- How might you adjust your expectations in your classroom? Be more specific? Add some expectations?

- Consider the time in the beginning of the class to introduce and teach the PBEs. How long would it take to begin each day teaching one PBE and to do so for 5 days?

Quick Wins

- Develop a list of academic expectations for your classroom:
  - Think critically
  - Collaborate
  - Communicate
  - Think creatively
  - Problem-solve
  - Work independently
  - Assess your peers
  - Assess your own work

- Develop your own rationale for each behavior and academic expectation.

- Have students come up with their own rationale for each expectation.

- Display expectations—student-created posters, videos, pictures of students exhibiting the behavior.

- Begin to think about potential levels of consequences, beginning with the least severe and ending with the most severe consequence.

3

Redirect Behavior Model

I was petrified. I never knew what to say to the students. During my first practicum experience as a pre-service teacher, I had little experience and it was quite evident to the students at that time. There were a couple of students I knew that would challenge me, not do what I asked them to do. So I did what every novice teacher would do: I avoided them. If I did address them when they were being disruptive, I thought that time had stood still. All I saw were their eyes, waiting for me to say something profound. Those words never came until Dr. Lentfer taught us how to address disruptive students. She taught us the Redirect Behavior Model.

We practiced the model before we went out for our second practicum. Just having that model and knowing that I will know what to say when a student isn't doing what they need to do, gave me a sense of relief. Not only did it work in the classroom, but it worked with my job and even with my boyfriend. At first it was uncomfortable, but as I kept practicing it became very conversational. I work in customer service and I use it all the time to calm customers down when they are angry. I love it!

Sarah Bohrer,
middle level language arts

Redirect Behavior Model Defined

The Redirect Behavior Model (RBM) is a proactive communication model for teachers to respectfully, and calmly, redirect inappropriate student behavior. It is a scripted guide that teachers can easily follow and implement in the classroom. The model is used with students Pre-K–12, and adults as well.

The premise for developing the model was to effectively communicate Positive Behavior Expectations (PBEs) while concentrating on appropriate communication skills in order to maintain a positive culture. Successful schools have concentrated on developing students' social interactions with the idea that the students will ultimately be able to self-regulate their actions. The Redirect Behavior Model aims to assist teachers in helping their students develop appropriate communication skills so that the students are able to manage their decision making successfully (Lentfer & Franks, 2015).

A panel of experts from the Institute of Education Sciences (2012) strongly recommended that teachers intentionally teach appropriate behavior and social skills throughout the curriculum. A number of studies have found behavior and social skills interventions dramatically decrease class disruptions, leading students to have more time on task (Institute of Education Sciences, 2012). Based on this research, RBM was developed to address effective communication for teachers to maintain a calm, productive classroom.

An ideal classroom climate occurs when teachers and students demonstrate respectful communication, low levels of disruption, and high levels of focus on tasks (La Paro & Pianta, 2003). When teachers lack the knowledge and skills for managing social and emotional situations, students will often demonstrate higher levels of disruptive and off-task behavior (Marzano, Marzano, & Pickering, 2003). Under these deteriorating conditions, teachers are easily frustrated; they often resort to reactive conditioned responses and do not teach the appropriate behavior and communication responses (Osher, Sprague, Weissberg, Axelrod, Keenan, Kendziora, & Zins, 2007). In addition, teachers are often at risk of becoming cynical and insensitive to students' needs.

When communication is effective, it benefits both teacher and student. Effective communication makes it easier for learning, has a positive effect on student achievement, strengthens the teacher–student relationship, and creates a positive community culture. The teacher who is able to communicate both verbally and nonverbally will be able to enhance the rapport with students and have a positive impact on student achievement. Effective communication is critical to the success of the student, whether it is verbal, nonverbal, individual, or in a whole-group setting.

The Redirect Behavior Model is instrumental in de-escalating potential volatile situations. The teacher offers the student positive and negative choices, which ultimately holds the student accountable to self-correct and regulate their own behavior. When a student is disruptive in the classroom, the student chooses which direction they want to take with their behavior. By placing accountability on the student, the teacher can remain calm and in control.

Empower Students

Educational empowerment studies—in particular, Perkins and Zimmerman (1995)—agree that empowerment is a belief in the ability to control conditions in one's circumstances. It is a certain level of autonomy and the individual's ability to determine their destiny in a responsible way. This includes a heightened sense of exerting self-control and an ability to critically understand one's surroundings. These abilities enable students and teachers to influence a positive change (Zimmerman, 1995). Empowerment characteristics that may exist include (1) clarity of expectations; (2) support from authority; (3) support from peers; (4) a strong sense of community; (5) access to resources; (6) inspired leadership; and (7) shared vision and values (Maton & Salem, 1995; Spreitzer, 1995).

Empowering students is at the very center of the framework for RBM. The framework is designed to empower students based on student choice, rationale, and value statements. Giving students decision-making power in the area of behavior may appear to be risky. However, the model, along with PBEs, informs the student of their choices and the consequences based on their decision.

Here are some ideas to begin empowering students:

- *Meaningfulness.* Discuss the rationale for their decisions.

- *Competence.* Tell them they are capable of performing the behavior appropriately.

- *Impact.* Connect real life to how their decision impacts their learning, classroom community, and personal life.

- *Choice.* If we make the classroom only about rules, how can we expect them to emerge as critical thinkers?

Teachers play an important role in creating an environment that fosters confidence in their students so they are then able to exhibit positive behavior. Through time the teacher will gradually release their role in addressing behavior and motivate students to be held accountable for their behavior. Teachers' confidence in their own ability is essential in transferring the power of choice over to the student. If a teacher understands that failure is temporary, yet necessary for success, they will be more likely to empower the student through choices.

FIGURE 3.1   How the Redirect Behavior Model Empowers Students

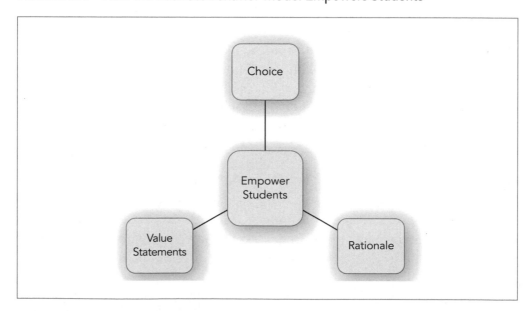

Framework of the Redirect Behavior Model

The Redirect Behavior Model's intent is to empower students (see Figure 3.1). The teacher will communicate a series of value statements, letting the student know they are valued and wanted in the classroom. The teacher will also offer a rationale as to why it's important to display positive behavior—which leads the student to have the autonomy in their choice. The teacher will guide students through this process by letting them know their choices. There are positive and negative choices, but the student is the one who chooses their destiny. Through the power of choice, and the value statements and rationale for appropriate behavior, the student will then be able to make their decision.

The Redirect Behavior Model's design is based upon three concepts:

1. *Value statements.* Let students know you value them.

2. *Rationale.* Offer a rationale for why you expect positive behavior.

3. *Choices.* Give students choices to self-correct their behavior.

Value Statements

Students have to know you care about them and want them in your classroom. This is especially important for students who may present more challenging behaviors. Some students may come to you with a pattern of getting kicked out of the classroom on a regular basis. Often, these students may feel teachers don't value or understand their needs. So it is of great importance that you make all of your students feel valued and that you want them to stay in your classroom. Would you work well for someone who may show in words or actions that they do not want you in their classroom? No. Everyone wants to feel valued and appreciated. When you take the time to let a student know they are valued and appreciated, the payoff is well worth the time in letting a student know how much you appreciate their efforts.

Rationale

The first question students pose after a redirection is, "Why do I have to . . . ?" Offering a rationale as you redirect student behavior will diminish the opportunity for students to argue with the teacher. Teaching to the *why* is at the very base of teaching. We address the *why* in content; we address the *why* in behavior.

Choices

This is the most powerful piece of RBM. The teacher transfers the power to the student by offering choices. It allows the students to be accountable for their actions. No one can make anyone do anything they do not want to do. I can't make a person drink a Pepsi if they really want a Coke. Both offer a sweet taste and can be quite appealing, but I can't force someone to do anything, no matter the circumstance. Offering choices regarding their behavior will allow the student to make good choices and do the right thing. Teachers may have to guide the conversation regarding choices. The teacher may have to offer the choices and then have the students ponder them.

The Redirect Behavior Model is a guided script that allows the teacher to respectfully redirect inappropriate behavior. It consists of three phases, as shown in the explanation that follows.

The Redirect Behavior Model

Phase I: Explain Student Behavior Expectations

(Teacher-Centered) Primarily used during the first month of school. The teacher teaches Positive Behavior Expectations (PBEs) and positive choices students can use to facilitate their learning.

Student Behavior Expectations

- **Value Statement:** *I understand . . .*
- **Acceptable Behavior:** *But I need you to . . .*
- **Rationale:** *Because . . .*
- **Time:** *Self-correct*
- **Noncompliant:** *Student choice—self-correct/consequence*
- **Time:** *Choose consequence*

After you have redirected the student using Phase I and the student was compliant, make sure to praise their improved behavior. However, after a short time the student may go back to the behavior you addressed previously; this is when you give the student choices—for example, if as a class you agreed there should be no cell phone use during instruction and a student is on their phone during instruction. The teacher approaches the student and uses Phase I. The student complies and the teacher moves on with the lesson. After a short time the student is back on their phone. The teacher will approach the student with choices and address the student in a quiet, calm voice and physically meet them at eye level (kneel down if the student is sitting). It may sound like this: *John, we talked about your phone use. We have a couple of choices here: You can (1) self-correct and participate with the rest of the class, or (2) you can continue your behavior. But there will be consequences for your behavior. I'll give you some time to think about your choices.* The teacher will then move away to give the student space to make their choice. Giving the student time and space will mitigate the power struggle.

Phase II: Encourage Student Ownership

(Student-Centered) Students are now aware of the expectations. When disruptions occur, the teacher asks a series of questions and provides students with choices so they can self-correct their behavior.

Student Ownership

Unacceptable Behavior: *What are you doing?*

Acceptable Behavior: *What should you be doing?*

Rationale: *Why do you think it's important?*

Time: Self-correct

Noncompliant: Student choice—Self-correct/consequence

If a student is noncompliant, give them a choice, and then they will either self-correct or they will need to receive the consequence of their choice.

Time: Choose consequence

Phase III: Problem-Solve With the Noncompliant Student

(Student-Centered) This is implemented only when students continue to require behavioral correction. The teacher provides the student with choices so they can self-correct their behavior. The student will either self-correct or continue the disruptive behavior. The continuation of disruptive behavior will result in consequences that are more serious.

Noncompliant

Choices: Easy or hard way

Acceptable Behavior: *You can self-correct and* [identify acceptable behavior], *OR*

Unacceptable Behavior: *You can continue to* [identify unacceptable behavior]

Consequences: Identify consequences

Time: *But I'm going to give you time to think about your choices*

Compliant: Praise for making a good choice

Noncompliant: Consequence—follow through maintaining a CALM demeanor

Implementing the Phases of the Redirect Behavior Model

The main objective of RBM is to establish and model the appropriate behavior that is expected throughout the school year. The teacher is teaching the behavior and guiding the redirection throughout each lesson. It is time intensive in the beginning, but students quickly learn the behavior expectations. Students also understand that you mean business because you address all the behaviors. Students quickly pick up on the behaviors and the fact that you (the teacher) will follow through with addressing all behaviors. Students want to be held accountable and will respect you a great deal more if you do follow through with each redirection.

The first phase is based on establishing the behavior expectations by teaching how to execute the behavior expectation and why that particular behavior is important. The teacher is at the center of teaching every behavior by modeling, addressing, and following through with each interaction.

I thought this was very easy to implement in the elementary classroom. This really supported my expectations and provided something for me to be able to explain what and why I needed the students to do something.

Aimi Asanuma,
pre-service elementary

Phase I: Explain Student Behavior Expectations

- When disruptions occur, calmly use the opportunity to teach PBEs to the whole class.

- Respond to the disruption in a structured, consistent manner.

- State why you want the student to remain in the classroom and be successful.

- Explicitly inform the student what you need them to do and how you need them to correct their behavior.

- Provide a rationale as to why it is important for them to perform the action or behavior.

- Offer the student the opportunity to choose to behave as you requested. Do not expect them to choose immediately. Let them know they have a few minutes to consider their choices.

- Walk away and resume teaching. Do not linger or hover over the student, waiting for a decision. Walking away diminishes the power struggle and allows the student to be accountable without losing their dignity.

- If the student chooses to self-correct, then consider the issue resolved.

- Take a moment to praise the student for self-correcting and making the right choice. Praise is an important component in reinforcing acceptable behavior.

I began to use Phase I with my high school students and they responded very well. They didn't question me and they went to work right away. The best part was that I didn't have to repeat myself because I gave them a rationale. I couldn't believe it, it absolutely worked! The more I used it the more natural it became to me.

Jessica Silknitter,
pre-service middle level

An example script for Phase I is:

Value Statement: *I understand you may not want to* ____ [appropriate behavior].

Acceptable Behavior: *But I need you to* ____ [specific behavior expectation].

Rationale: *The reason why it's important to* ____ [specific behavior expectation] ____ *is because* ____ [rationale—real-life application].

Time: For student to self-correct

Noncompliant: Student choice—self-correct/consequences

- If the student repeats the behavior, go over to the student (on their eye level), and say in a calm voice:

We talked about ____ [state the behavior]. *You have a couple of choices. You can self-correct or you can continue your behavior, but know that there are consequences. I'm going to give you a couple of minutes to think about your choices.*

Time: Choose consequences (student)

- Promptly move away from the student. This will give the student time to think and not feel pressure. This will also assist to de-escalate any power struggle.

Phase I: Noncompliance—What to Do if a Student Does Not Accept the Redirection

- If the student continues to display the disruptive behavior, go over to the student (proximity) and let them know you still value them.

- Use a calm, quiet voice and physically get on their eye level. If the student is sitting, kneel down to talk with them.

- Say, *We talked about your behavior and we have some choices going forward. You can self-correct and continue with your classmates, or you can continue to do what you are doing. But remember there are consequences* [a call home, go to partner teacher's room and complete a behavior action plan, etc.] *for your actions.*

The best part of RBM is that it takes the responsibility off of the teacher's shoulders and transfers it to the student. It alleviates the burden of needing to fix the situation. The situation naturally fixes itself through conversation and choices.

> After communicating their choices, immediately walk away to give them time to consider their potential outcomes regarding their choices.

Use Phase I primarily during the first 2 weeks. Reiterate your behavior expectations and content expectations using Phase I. You do not always have to use this for disruptive behavior. For example, use it to introduce content.

Teacher: *Value Statement*: I understand that sometimes students have difficulty understanding fractions. I know it was difficult for me.

Acceptable Behavior: But I need you to take notes as we work through some of the different methods to solving these problems.

Rationale: If we do this together and write down each step we can use our notes for reference as we work with a partner using manipulatives.

Notice in the preceding example that the teacher addressed the whole class and clearly communicated exactly what they needed to do to accomplish a task.

Phase II: Encourage Student Ownership

Phase II of RBM is student-centered. The students take on a more participatory role during the interaction and learn to take responsibility for their behavior. The teacher serves as the facilitator during the redirection, utilizing a series of questions that will redirect the student to make better choices.

Phase II questions to encourage student ownership:

- What are you doing?

- What should you be doing?

- Why is this important?

- How does that impact you?

- What are you going to choose to do?

An example script of Phase II—Encourage Student Ownership is:

Student Identifies Unacceptable Behavior: *Betsy, what are you doing?* (Student identifies disruptive behavior.)

Student Identifies Acceptable Behavior: *What should you be doing?* (Student identifies appropriate behavior.)

Student Identifies Rationale: *Why do you think that would benefit you?* (Student identifies rationale; may have to help identify a real-life connection rationale.)

Self-Correct: Give time for student to self-correct.

Noncompliant: Student choice—self-correct/consequence.

Time: Choose consequence.

I was teaching a lesson during my practicum. I was still in the beginning stages of getting to know the students. I had asked the whole class to take notes during my instruction. There was a student in the back who did not take notes. In fact, he sat in the back with his headphones on, staring at his phone. My mentor teacher does not allow students to be on their phones or use headphones. This particular student would always be on his phone with headphones and my teacher always had to ask him to put them away every day. So I knew that I had to redirect his behavior. I went to the back of the room to talk to him.

At first I was a little scared, but Dr. Lentfer had us practice Phase I and II a ton so it luckily came out pretty smooth. I told him that I understood that being on the phone was much more fun than taking notes, but that I needed him to put it away so he wouldn't fall behind. I waited for him, heart pounding, but he did what I asked him to do, albeit slowly.

A few minutes later he put one earbud back in to listen to whatever was on his phone. I had just started the students working in partners, so I went back to talk to him again. This time I asked him what he was doing. He said that he was doing nothing. I asked, "What should you be doing?" And he mumbled that he needed to work with a partner. I agreed and asked him what he should do about his earbuds. He said he needed to put them away. I told him great! That's a great choice because his partner really needed his help with the assignment. I asked if he thought I should take his phone so it wouldn't be tempting him to use it. He thought that I wouldn't have to do that. I told him great, but if I had to talk to him again about his earbuds we were going to talk about some of the choices he would have going forward.

It helped me to have something I could say to a student that I didn't know very well. I knew eventually if I had to give him choices that it would take the responsibility off of me.

Emilie Wolfe,
middle level math and science

After I established the Positive Behavior Expectations the class was moving along quite well. The classroom culture was a positive, supportive environment. I was able to redirect my students using Phase II. The students responded well and I was able to dig deeper into the content and integrate more collaborative group activities.

Daniel Stokes,
science, Grades 7–12

Phase II of the Redirect Behavior Model was easier to implement and allowed the students to be involved in the redirection. The rationale supported the why, so students wouldn't argue. And I knew I could ask them, "Why do you think it's important to do this?"

Emma Tuttle,
pre-service elementary

Phase III: Problem-Solve With the Noncompliant Student

Phase III is directed toward the student who has had several interactions. They are the repeat offenders. The teacher has informed the parent(s) consistently, teachers have met regarding the student behavior, and administrators have been informed as well. The teacher has employed multiple consequences over an extended period of time, yet the student continues to display inappropriate behavior. The teacher is firm in the delivery as well as the message. The student is presented with choices, but the consequence is a little more severe. The consequence is to be removed from the room. Again, the teacher informs the student of their choices and walks away to give them time to ponder them. If the student chooses not to correct their behavior, the teacher, in a calm manner, will give them a referral to go to the dean's office. Phase III is the last resort. However, I rarely had to employ Phase III. In fact, I may have sent a student to the office once a year. I was persistent in working with students in understanding and displaying appropriate behavior. I wanted the students to remain in my classroom. I knew they would miss out on so much instruction that it would be detrimental to their future. I felt that if they were out of my classroom they would be missing opportunities to learn social and academic skills.

Also, elementary teachers may have to indicate their choices and the consequences. This is more teacher-centered and direct communication. You as the teacher need to take more of the control at this level. State the choices and consequences with a firm voice tone and do not allow the student to argue. This is the level where you have had several conversations, phone calls home, and the administration is well aware of the situation. It should be no surprise to the student that you are going to be firm, but fair.

An example script to use in Phase III is:

Choices: *Betsy, you can choose to* _____ [acceptable behavior] *or choose to continue* _____ [unacceptable behavior].

Acceptable Behavior: *You can* _____ [identify acceptable behavior] *and we can get our work done and everyone in the classroom is happy* [could give a real-life application, e.g., no homework], *OR*

Unacceptable Behavior: *You can continue* _____ [identify unacceptable behavior], *you'll be sent to the dean's office, and we will have to inform your parents, principal, assistant principal, and guidance counselor about your behavior. You'll end up having a ton of homework because you'll miss out on time to get your work done, you'll be behind, and you'll have to come in after school to get caught up.*

Time: *Think about the choice—don't answer right away. I see that you are quite upset right now. I'm going to give you a few minutes to think about this decision* [dependent on the intensity of situation].

You're giving the student a chance to save face. It will de-escalate the situation and allow the student to calm themselves.

Compliant–Self-Correct: If the student begins participating, even if it is a little, leave them alone. Give them a chance to self-correct. Praise them with value statements.

Noncompliant–Consequence: *Okay, you made your decision.* Do not hesitate. Follow through with the consequence. Don't give in and give them a chance, especially if this is the first Phase III you encountered in the class. It sends a very strong message to the class that you are serious about your expectations *and* follow-through.

Remember to remain CALM while delivering this message!

> *I had been working with a student on how to begin an assignment. She hadn't used the time in class to complete her assignments, therefore she did not turn in her work, and her grade was suffering due to the lack of effort in the classroom. I kept in contact with her parents via email and phone conversations. They were very much aware of the situation, but I had to prompt her often during class to begin her assignment and to refrain from talking during independent work time. After I prompted her to begin her assignment, she refused to follow my instruction. I went over to her and told her that we have a couple of choices, you can self-correct or you can continue your behavior, but you know the consequences. Since she displayed this behavior frequently and I had multiple contacts with her parents regarding her behavior, I gave her an opportunity to see me before school the next day to develop some solutions. She accepted quietly and we did come up with some strategies that would help her be successful.*
>
> Michaela Kavanagh,
> high school, business

Follow-Through

Follow-through is often abandoned if the student is able to self-correct. However, it is of high importance to take a moment and praise the student for self-correcting and making the right choice. Praise is an important component in reinforcing acceptable behavior.

It is absolutely critical for teachers to follow through with established consequences when students continue to display noncompliant behavior. Following through establishes boundaries and teaches students that their choices have consequences. Deliver the consequences in a calm tone, without emotion. State the consequences as a matter of fact and deliver the message with a calm tone. Take the emotions out of the equation, trust the process, and remain firm on the consequence.

> *I was using the Redirect Behavior Model and was having success; however, I still felt like my students were repeating the same behaviors. I decided to record myself over a short period of time. After I reviewed the recordings I noticed I implemented RBM and incorporated the behavior expectations just fine. But I wasn't following through conversations about modifying behavior. I simply made a phone call home or had them stay after school in our detention room. Once I had those conversations, behavior improved and I began to develop stronger relationships with my students.*
>
> Amy Nguyen,
> high school, world languages

> *This is the piece (follow through) I really had to work on. I didn't want my students to think I was mean. But I realized that if I didn't follow through with the consequences the behavior would not change.*
>
> Ben Carder,
> middle level math

Delivering the Redirect Behavior Model

It can take some time for RBM to feel natural for you. Here are some tips to remember as you practice. Before long, both you and your students will adjust to these routines. Use a calm, conversational tone while addressing students.

Say It and Move On

When implementing RBM, it is imperative that you implement the phase and move on, especially if the student appears to be agitated easily. With the exception of Phase III, where you give the student time to think about their choices, you don't want to spend any additional time beyond the script. Giving the behavior and student additional attention beyond the script can immediately escalate the situation into a power struggle between the teacher and the student. In addition, it takes time away from classroom instruction.

> *At first it was uncomfortable delivering the Redirect Behavior Model. It seemed scripted, but the more I practiced it became easier. It really allowed me to explain things in a simple, easy to understand way.*
>
> Jessica Sorrell,
> middle level science

> *I had a power struggle with a student. He was doing nothing during our independent work time. I asked him to get his notebook out and start writing. He said he didn't want to. I then demanded him to get his notebook out: wrong. He persisted not to get out his notebook. I sat down next to him and had a conversation and explained what I needed him to do. I walked away, but he never started writing; instead, he pushed the notebook away and started watching YouTube on his iPad. I left him alone for a few minutes, then went back to him, knelt down by him, and this time I gave him a couple of options: You can either get on IXL and work on your two skills from last week or you can write about the video we just watched. I'll give you some time to think about your choices. I walked away. This time, he laid his head down for about 10 seconds. I just gave him the time, and then he started to get onto IXL on his iPad. I felt so proud!! I then went over with a sticky note, complimenting him on his choice, and thanked him for getting started.*
>
> Sarah Bohrer,
> middle level language arts

Make It Conversational

The Redirect Behavior Model is a script, but it should not sound like a script. The goal is to make it sound natural, as if you were having a conversation with the student (because you are!). With practice your efficacy will increase, and it will sound and feel much more like a conversation. Practice Phase I outside of the classroom. Use the model with your children, significant other, friends, even your pet.

Keep in mind that the model is just a guide. You do not have to follow the script verbatim. It is important to practice the model with the idea of incorporating each component for each phase with proficiency. Cognitively, you will have each component, so if there is a challenging situation you are able to retrieve the main components of the script.

> *Using RBM helped me to teach students to be in charge of their own learning. I wanted them to begin to make better choices. The more I used the model, the more confidence I had in addressing behavior. I practiced at home and with my friends, and it became more conversational. I was able to give them choices through a conversation. It was awesome!*
>
> Sarah Bohrer,
> middle level language arts

Be Prepared for Students to Feel Uncomfortable

Remember, this may be a new way for students to communicate. Students may react a little different toward you at first. Their reaction may give an impression such as *this is crazy or strange,* or *why are you talking to me like that?* Courage is a must when entering this unknown territory. Be strong; the students will quickly acquiesce to your requests. You are establishing your behavior expectations and a culture of respect. It is imperative that you stay the course and persevere through the potentially uncomfortable moments. Change does not come without a few growing pains. Be consistent, follow through; the more you practice, the more it becomes conversational. After practicing you'll have a whole new presence in the classroom.

Students may be uncomfortable when they are first presented with choices, a rationale, and value statements. They may roll their eyes or communicate either verbally or nonverbally that they don't know how to react to someone speaking to them in this way. It may take some students longer truly to understand how to communicate with respect. If a student admonishes the model, this is exactly the signal to let you know that that is precisely what this student needs. Stay strong!

The delivery of RBM is just as important as the words that are spoken. Practicing the model at length is required to ensure a smooth, conversational tone. Since RBM is scripted, at first glance, the model may come across as uncomfortable. However, with practice the model will become automatic and more conversational.

> When I first used this in class I thought it sounded too scripted. I was not comfortable using it, but Dr. Lentfer encouraged us to practice with our significant other, family, friends, even our pet. The more I used it the more it sounded like a conversation. I used it in my classroom and it worked! Students didn't argue and they followed my instruction. And if a student continued, I would give them choices. It helped with my confidence and it gave something to say to the students. I always heard teachers tell students to sit down and stop talking. This actually addressed the behavior in a conversational tone.
>
> Katie Nice,
> special education, Grades K–12

> The Redirect Behavior Model taught to me was very effective, not only inside the classroom, but even at home with my children. Dr. Lentfer's RBM strategies have proven to have a positive tone to them while accomplishing proper redirection. As I have alluded to, using her techniques even when redirecting my children produces a positive result.
>
> Chancy Sims,
> high school, business

Remain Calm

Staying calm is essential in communicating that you are in control of your emotions and you are not going to the level of anger the misbehaving student is displaying. Often, an upset student will try to engage an authority figure in arguing over the rules or the misbehavior displayed. Their goal is to get the attention off of them and their behavior. The student will try to divert the attention of the teacher to someone or something else, or to blame others for their actions so they are not accountable for their behavior.

Take a look at the following scenario (note how the teacher uses Phase II of RBM to address the student in a calm manner):

> *John is a seventh-grade student in an algebra class. This is the third month into the semester, so the Positive Behavior Expectations (PBEs) have been well established. The class expectation is no cell phone use during instruction. John tends to exhibit off-task behavior and uses his cell phone during instruction. John begins to text while the teacher is instructing.*
>
> **Teacher:** John, what are you doing?
>
> **John:** Texting.
>
> **Teacher:** What should you be doing?
>
> **John:** Listening.
>
> **Teacher:** Why are you using your cell phone while I am instructing?
>
> **John:** Because a friend texted me.
>
> **Teacher:** Is there an emergency?
>
> **John:** No, but it isn't my fault a friend texted me.
>
> **Teacher:** As a class, what did we agree upon with the use of cell phones during instruction?
>
> **John:** To not use them.
>
> **Teacher:** So, what do you think you should do with the cell phone?
>
> **John:** But it isn't my fault that my friend is texting me.
>
> **Teacher:** I understand it isn't your fault your friend is texting you, but we agreed as a class to put our phones away during instruction. Do you think you can do that?
>
> **John:** Yes.
>
> **Teacher:** Great! Thank you for accepting feedback.

Students can try to manipulate a situation by transferring their responsibility onto someone else. A teacher has to remain focused on the specific disruption. John tried to place blame on his friend for texting him, which John used as a way to validate his being on the cell phone. As the scenario showed, it is appropriate to acknowledge that as a class we agreed to put away cell phones during instruction. The teacher has to remain on topic and redirect the behavior that appears to be instigating the interruption.

It is important not to engage in arguing with a student. This is why it is imperative to have a PBE addressing arguing and the appropriate steps to disagree (see Chapter 2).

Now, if you feel that two students are equally guilty of being disruptive, it is appropriate to let both of the students know that talking is not okay during instruction and you will address this situation during work time (or at a later time, but within the next 24–48 hours). This gives everyone a chance to approach the situation in a calm manner and will allow the teacher to consider all sides, have a conversation with both parties, and have a peaceful resolution. Taking that moment to gather your thoughts so you are able to remain calm during the corrective conversation will allow you to manage your emotions so there can be a peaceful resolution.

Redirect Behavior Model for Instruction

The Redirect Behavior Model does not have to be limited to redirecting poor behavior. Phase I can also be used as a method of instruction. The model is a reflection of good teaching and good communication. During instruction

I frequently used Phase I of the Redirect Behavior Model while I addressed the whole class. I used it during an English composition class. The students were having difficulty writing an essay. At the time I was a pre-service college student, so I related a story of how I struggled with writing at times, but putting it off and not trying or attempting the assignment only made it worse. The fact that I needed to write essays did not go away, unless I didn't want to graduate. I went on to tell them I needed them to begin the process of writing. I empathized with them, told them what they needed to do, and gave a rationale. Not only did they work, but it helped to develop my relationship with the class.

Amanda Shurtliff,
English, Grades 7–12

you can indicate the value statement, choices, and rationale. Here are some examples of how this may be implemented:

Whole-Group Instruction

Teacher: *I know you may think that writing a 10-page research paper seems like it will be hard. I understand, it can be difficult.* (Value Statement)

But as a class we are going to take it step by step together. (Appropriate Behavior—what you need them to do)

If we take it step by step and you follow along, then it won't be so overwhelming and you will feel better about accomplishing something you didn't think you could do. (Rationale)

Using RBM for instruction is another way to practice having these conversations with your students so that they're familiar with the norms and expectations when there are disruptions from behavior.

Summary

The Redirect Behavior Model is a respectful conversational communication tool to redirect student behavior. It empowers the student through choices and places the responsibility on the student regarding their choices. It can be used for instruction and redirecting inappropriate behavior. It is a straightforward guide to sound communication.

Reflection Questions

- Have you ever found yourself in a confrontation with a student and you didn't know what to say? How did that make you feel? How did the situation turn out? How could RBM de-escalate the situation?

- Think about a time when a student tried to argue over why they had to do something. How would RBM be able to navigate this situation?

- Think about a time when a situation began to escalate between you and a student. Did you raise your voice? Use threatening words? How did the student react? How could RBM have helped you to control your emotions and remain calm?

Quick Wins

- Practice Phase I with your significant other, children, friends, coworkers, and even your pet. The more you practice the more it will become natural and conversational.

- Reflect on how the students, family, etc., reacted when you used Phase I.

- How did you feel when you delivered the model? Did you feel more comfortable the more times you used the model?

- Continue to practice and reflect if there is a difference in delivery and an increase in confidence.

- Try recording yourself using the model. Note your voice tone, the student's reaction: Was it conversational? Did you begin with value statements? State the rationale. State the choices. Pick one item to improve. Record yourself again and check to see if you improved. Continue this process until you feel you are completely confident in the delivery.

Voice-Movement-Task Model

When I was teaching seventh-grade math, I incorporated small-group work activities. The small groups worked fairly well. Students completed their work, worked together, and learned from one another. Sounds like a success, right? Well, yes and no. The students worked well, but I often felt like I was doing a disproportionate amount of work. Whether I was helping with the task by answering questions, or consumed with classroom management by prompting groups to stay on task, keep their hands to themselves, refrain from off-topic talking, or keep their voices low, I was constantly reacting instead of leading. To address this problem head on, I decided to videotape my classroom during small-group work. Several themes emerged from my video analysis.

First, I noticed I addressed voice levels often. It was a reactive method of addressing behavior. Second, the students didn't always stay within their group and often did not have the appropriate materials. I would tell the students what materials they needed as they moved into their groups. This was futile because they weren't listening; they were busy moving into their groups. Even if they were listening to me, they couldn't hear me because the sound level was too high. I would repeat myself several times while they were moving (they couldn't hear me); and when they finally did get into their groups, I had to repeat myself several times again because that caused more sound from more movement from students returning to their seats to get their materials. I then noticed that when students moved they often wasted time talking to other students, they didn't go directly to their seats, and they often touched or messed with other people's materials. Third, the recording revealed that I would give the long list of directions, and when the students were ready to begin their task I would go around in a panicked frenzy retelling the directions to each group. The directions were so unclear even when I personally addressed each group that I then had to spend more time showing them how to get started and explain why this activity worked with the content. I was a mess by the time I addressed all the questions regarding directions, materials, and the escalating voice levels.

My method was reactive; I wanted to be proactive. Students don't know what I expect until I tell them and show them what I expect. Thus, the Voice-Movement-Task Model emerged. I was going to address their voices, movement, and the material, and the directions were going to be very clear before we began to work in our small groups.

Voice-Movement-Task Model Defined

The Voice-Movement-Task Model (VMT) is a proactive communication model that addresses specific behavior expectations prior to every lesson or cooperative learning activity. The model strengthens teacher communication and minimizes student disruption to provide a safe, productive classroom environment. It is a straightforward guideline that addresses the three areas that present the most disruption: voices, movement, and task instructions. It has been well documented that a lack of classroom control leads to the inability of teachers to teach and students to learn (Ratcliffe, Carroll, & Hunt, 2014). Preventative measures such as communicating behavior expectations ahead of time have the potential to decrease disruptions, off-task behavior, and opportunities for bullying.

Instructional Advantage

The Voice-Movement-Task Model is a critical element within the instructional framework. The model allows for efficient transitions, clear expectations, and directions, which provide more time for instruction. Teachers are able to be more efficient with their time in managing behavior and concentrating on instruction. This model enhances the teacher's ability to deliver lessons that maximize student engagement and learning. It is an effective guide for Pre-K–12 teachers and students.

Implementing the Voice-Movement-Task Model allowed me to have more time to dive into instruction. I didn't have to worry about the behaviors or the directions because the model really helped the students to know the expectations. It also helped me to stay organized as well.

Ben Carder,
middle level math

FIGURE 4.1   The Voice-Movement-Task Model

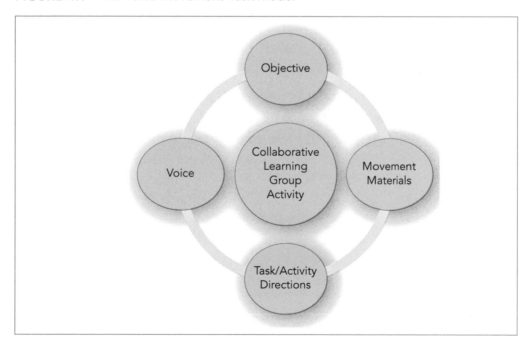

Research

Behavior management has evolved and transformed as the diverse demands of the social and behavioral landscape have changed. By setting aside time before the lesson begins to communicate behavior expectations, learning expectations, success criteria, and the task protocol, teachers will be able to increase the time on task. An instructional approach that is reactive disrupts the flow of the lesson and reduces the learning time for all of the students in the classroom. Researchers have found the more a teacher is able to communicate clear and concise behavior expectations, the more chances the students will have to be able to meet and exceed those behavior expectations (Evertson, Emmer, & Worsham, 2006; Marzano, 2010; McKown & Weinstein, 2008; Zirpoli, 2008).

When to Use

The optimal time to implement VMT is prior to a collaborative work-group activity. The main function is to prepare the students to be successful by indicating the appropriate behaviors for the activity.

When you first introduce VMT to your class you will want to demonstrate each area of the model. Plan for a little extra time to do this. Each successive time you use VMT you will spend less time modeling the expectations.

Voice

There are four voice levels:

- Level 0
  - No talking
- Level 1
  - Partner talk
  - Whisper

- Level 2
  - ○ Small group
  - ○ Loud enough for your small group to hear, but not loud enough to disrupt the classes next door or across the hall
- Level 3
  - ○ Whole-group discussion
  - ○ Loud enough for your small group to hear, but not loud enough to disrupt the classes next door or across the hall

The voice levels, once established, may be used at other times as well, not just during collaborative working group activities. Students will be aware of the voice levels and respond accordingly when prompted with a specific voice level request. Once you introduce the voice levels, students grasp onto the concept fairly well. The voice levels are fairly straightforward, but they are also a great way to prompt students throughout class if they are getting too loud. Eventually, you will just need to prompt them with "Voices!" and the students will self-correct. It is worth the time to be able to get there!

When I first introduced VMT, I only had one behavior expectation for voice and movement. I didn't want to overwhelm my students. And I wanted to take the time for the students to practice the expectation before we did our literacy circles.

Aimi Asanuma,
pre-service elementary

Progression Adjustments

Again, teaching behavior is equivalent to teaching content. For example, if students are able to calculate a one-step equation, the teacher will then begin to challenge them and move onto the next concept. So, if students are able to employ the expectations with a high level of proficiency, adjust the expectations to a higher level. Meet the students where they are regarding their behavior.

Elementary School

Basic Expectation: Voice levels

Next Step Up: One person at a time will talk; listen to your partner without interrupting

Higher Level: Sentence starters, e.g., *I like that you* . . . Helpful comments versus hurtful comments

Middle School

Basic Expectation: Voice levels

Next Step Up: On-topic conversations during small group

Higher Level: Positive and supportive comments to each member of their small group

All members are able to employ PBEs regarding small-group conversations

High School

Basic Expectation: Voice levels

Next Step Up: On-topic conversations during small group

Higher Level: Positive and supportive comments to each member of their small group

All members are able to employ PBEs regarding small-group conversations.

The progression for middle and high school students should focus on communication and how to empower students to have a productive, supportive conversation. The challenge for secondary students is to engage in appropriate conversation. Unfortunately, it is while working in small groups that students may be harassed or bullied. Communicating your expectations is foundational in preventing potential harassment or bullying situations. You may have to practice how to have appropriate conversations.

Some of the expectations for positive discourse may include:

- Maintain on-topic conversations
- Make supportive comments—especially if the topic is sensitive or for challenging material
- No "put-downs" or judging others for their mistakes
- Make this a judgment-free zone
- Listen to others' opinions and ideas
- Everyone is able to share their ideas

When I had to introduce the voice levels in my classroom, I was able to use the VMT method to guide my instruction. If I did not address behavior expectations and make the activity directions clear and concise, I would have a ton of questions and redirections. The more I used the model, the better my students understood my expectations and knew that I was going to model and post my directions for the activity.

Katie Nice,
special education, Grades K–12

Adjust the expectations to the needs of the students. These will vary for each class. Voice is not limited to the varying voice levels; it addresses the PBEs regarding how to have small-group interactions and on-topic conversations. If there is a specific area of challenge students may be displaying, address the behavior prior to the activity.

> Meet your students where they are with their behavior. If they understand voice levels, prompt them to have on-topic conversations, not to talk across the room, to use supportive comments, and to converse with group members only.

Some voice adjustments may include:

- On-topic conversations
- No shouting or talking across the room
- Supportive comments for your team members
- Listen to all ideas
- Share ideas knowing that someone may not agree with your thoughts

Movement

1. Signal

Establish a signal for students to follow when their group needs to rotate. This could include when the music starts or stops; your personal attention-getter, for example, if you create a classroom mantra—the teacher may say "We are" and the students respond with Wilson Badgers (the name of their school and their mascot); lights on or off; or cowbell. The more creative the signal is, the more students will be willing to follow it. Take a risk and try singing your favorite commercial jingle or quoting a famous movie line.

2. Movement paths

Establish the direction in which the groups will rotate. Have the students practice before they engage in the activity. Place students into groups, ascertain that they understand the directions for the activity, and let them know what the signal is. Then have them rotate from one station to the next as a practice run before the activity begins. Once you have established the expectation for rotation, begin the activity.

Note: Once you establish the direction in which the groups will move (clockwise or counterclockwise), continue to expect groups to move in the same direction for future classroom activities. Keep the movement of the groups simple and routine.

3. Lining up

Lining up is a critical skill for elementary students to have because they use it regularly throughout the day. Students will need to line up, single file, to go to the restroom, recess, art class, gym, cafeteria, etc. Practice with your students to keep their hands and feet to themselves, with no talking. If you are walking in the hallway, indicate that they will need to walk on the right-hand side of the hall. Also, put line leaders in the front and back. Designate several stopping points in the hall where the front line leader can stop. This will give the students and teacher a chance to catch up and calmly go over the expectations again before moving on. Have one of the stopping points midway through each hall—the teacher should be able to see the line leader in the front. Choose stopping points that are easy for the students to identify, such as the water fountain, restrooms, or end of the hallway.

4. Maintaining classroom materials

Materials play a critical role in the learning environment. Addressing materials prior to the activity can eliminate questions regarding the procedures for students to hand in materials, transition time between activities, and prevent having the teacher clean the work spaces at the end of class. Have the students be responsible for cleaning their work space. Communicate the where, when, and how the students will need to handle the materials. Here are some material ideas to consider:

- Where and how to handle materials for classwork
- How to move to use the materials—e.g., gym, art, music
- Where to hand in the finished product
- Cleaning the work space
- Science lab materials/movement

Continue to hold students accountable for all of the established behavior expectations. Hold them accountable by having the students practice the expectation until they have displayed the appropriate behavior. If you requested them to have a voice level 0 and they were talking as they moved, make them go back to their original station, give them the signal, and have them rotate again. Even if they barely missed the mark on one of your expectations, have them go back to their station and review the VMT behavior expectations. Expect perfection. This sends a serious message to the students that you mean what you say and you are going to follow through with your expectations. Follow-through is key; have students repeat the movement until they have achieved your expectation. Having students practice until it's perfect will allow you to hold them to high expectations.

Materials

How many times have you given directions, divided students into groups, and sent them on their way to begin their task, only to find yourself reeling them back in to tell them what materials they need for the activity? Students may not be paying attention because they are excited and talking among themselves as they divide into their groups. So you begin to talk louder, your voice is lost in the tumult, and the students are confused: What do you want them to have for the activity? Now they have to start over and get the proper materials. You have lost both time and the students' focus.

Establishing norms on how and when to move materials will help eliminate much confusion and chaos in the classroom. Here are some examples of expectations for handling materials:

- Students need the following materials for activity—pen/pencil, paper, notes, textbook.

- Students need to move their materials (notes, drinks, textbooks) off the table or desk.

- Students need to move their backpacks under the desk.

- Students need to take all of their materials with them to their new small group.

- Students need to put their food/drinks away or their food and drinks may not be allowed.

- Students need to hand in their completed work on the front table.

- Students are responsible to clean their work space (pick up any trash on the floor, place materials away in their proper location, push in chairs).

- It is important to think through students' personal materials because if a student moves from their seat for the small-group activity, a number of things could happen. Someone may mess with their materials, or the perception of students messing with their materials may cause a negative confrontation or loss of instructional time, and may lead to further negative interactions. Also, having the students move their materials off the table or desk allows for more room to work and lessens the potential for distractions. Moving the materials (e.g., backpacks) out of the walking pathway will allow both teacher and students to move with ease without tripping over backpacks as they walk throughout the room. Plus, it just makes for a more organized, clean, and pleasant environment.

Task

The *T* in VMT pertains to the directions for the activity. There is an art and science to giving directions. It takes careful consideration and much preparation prior to executing a collaborative working group activity for it to be successful. Do not assume students understand what you want them to do, whether it pertains to academics or behavior. It would be negligent to overlook the impact directions have on productivity regarding academic tasks.

One time I had to list more expectations for the materials for a project that required using multiple pieces of material (glue, scissors, crayon, etc.). I really wanted to let them know the location of the materials and how to handle them, and finally how to clean up. We were using scissors and I didn't want them to get hurt. Plus, I'm a pre-service teacher and I wasn't sure if my mentor teacher taught them how to use the scissors. I just wanted to be sure.

Michael Stennis,
pre-service elementary

> Economy of words! Directions should only be 3–5 bullet points. Use pictures liberally.

Here are some ideas to consider when planning and giving directions:

* *Clarity*

    Directions should be straightforward. Delete any extra wording that could be confusing.

- *Concise*

  Don't get too wordy. Reassess your directions and try to cut extra words. Your 3–5 directions should be able to fit on one PowerPoint slide. Consider using bullet points.

- *Chronological*

  Directions should be a logical, step-by-step process.

- *Chunk and chew*

  If the activity is particularly long and complex and involves more than 5 steps, then chunk the steps into groups of five. Begin by giving students the first 5 steps (chunk). Once the students have completed those 5 (chew), then give them the next set of 5 steps. Repeat this process until all directions have been given. Students and adults alike have difficulty listening to more than 5 directions at a time.

- *Partner explanation*

  Have students turn to their partner and explain/discuss the expectations for the activity.

- *Use pictures to convey your message*

- *Rationale*

  State the purpose of following directions and the purpose of the activity.

- *Check for understanding*

  Discern if your students have properly internalized the directions. But do not assume that because you read the list of expectations and directions and discussed them that the students have internalized them. Here are some methods to consider when checking for understanding regarding the behavior expectations and activity directions:

  - *Visual:* Directions should be visually available.
  - *Verbal:* Teacher verbalizes; students may review with a partner.

- *Question:* Call upon students to restate expectations.

- *Written:* Have directions written on paper for each station.

- *Post:* Post on a PowerPoint, whiteboard, or SMART board. Have directions posted throughout the activity for easy reference.

- *Model:* Show how to participate in the activity.

- *Role-play:* Take the time to have students practice.

- *Restate directions:* Have students restate. This is especially beneficial for your English language learners and special education learners.

> Take the time to have students restate the directions. Ask the students:
>
> What is the first thing we are going to do? What's the second thing we are going to do? What do we do when we are finished?

Check for Understanding

Keep pacing in mind while reviewing the behavior expectations and activity directions. It is important to implement several of the methods to check for understanding, but be aware of your class. They are important to review, but don't belabor the points if it is evident the students are fully aware of the expectations.

Some of the behavior expectations will need to have students role-play or model the expectations in the beginning. But students are fairly quick to learn expectations, so role-playing and modeling may decrease with each activity. Plan for more time during the first few group activities to review expectations. Eventually, you may only need to do quick prompts for voice levels or movement. Having a strong understanding of your students' knowledge and skills is key to keeping the pace at an appropriate level.

> *The Voice-Movement-Task Model serves as a great reminder for student behavior because in a science lab, there could be some serious repercussions if they did not follow directions. My directions began to get better as a result of implementing the VMT. I have learned to have the directions posted in front of the class, at their lab stations, and we modeled the directions prior to the labs. As I became more proficient in designing my directions I began to integrate pictures, which I had fun making, and the students enjoyed the pictures. I used cartoons, which captured the students' attention. I didn't realize how directions had such a profound effect on the learning environment. The VMT helped to organize my thoughts and prepare my students for their labs. Now I look forward to my lab days!*
>
> Daniel Stokes,
> science, Grades 7–12

Quick Wins

Begin by posting the expectations for students to reference, but also for you. The Voice-Movement-Task Model is a proactive measure for students, but it also provides reminders for you, the teacher. It will help to keep you organized. This is an example of a PowerPoint slide I have used in my professional development workshop:

FIGURE 4.2   VMT Behavior Expectations

Behavior Expectations

Voice—Level 3

Movement—Stand in a Circle
                    Hands and Feet to Self

Task—Each person will share why they want to be a teacher
        After you share your story, toss the ball to another classmate
        Share your story when you have the ball
        Continue until everyone has shared their story

Instructional Advantage

We discussed how this maximizes instructional time. But it also provides a better understanding of the objective of the lesson. It allows the teacher to focus on engagement and not management.

Summary

The Voice-Movement-Task Model is a proactive measure to prepare students for success regarding their behavior and academic expectations prior to a lesson or an activity. It specifically addresses common areas of challenge for teachers and students: voice/talking, movement/materials, task/activity directions, and objective/what is the purpose of the lesson/activity. It's a guide for the student and teacher. It prompts teachers to prepare materials and manage their time according to the directions and expectations.

Reflection Questions

- Think about a time when you did not indicate the behavior expectations prior to a lesson or activity. Was your instructional time efficient? Did the students know exactly what they were supposed to do?

- Directions are often ignored, yet teachers tend to be frustrated with students following directions. How has the model helped in developing your skills in delivering directions?

Quick Wins

- Try to concentrate on improving your directions. Give your directions outside of your classroom or to friends or colleagues not associated with education. Ask if they are able to follow your directions.

(Continued)

(Continued)

- Try inserting photos that could take the place of two sentences or two bullet points. For example, to indicate whole-group discussion, consider using a picture of a tiger with its mouth wide open.

- Keep your pacing going—do not belabor the expectations. If your students are able to understand voice levels, prompt them to have on-topic conversations and supportive comments, without talking across the room.

- Use images liberally. You may use images to show each step of the process or what the final product may look like. This will guide the English language learners as well.

C
A
L
M

PART II

ACCOUNTABILITY

Accountability— Collaborative Work Groups

I had a student who seemed disengaged as a learner. He would sleep, was unprepared, and rarely turned in assignments. To get the student even to sit up took a great deal of prompting. I began to have conversations with the student. Through the conversations I began to understand him better. Once we were able to better understand one another and his situation, I was able to adjust my expectations and work with him. We started small and gradually increased the expectations. For example, we started with having him stay awake during class. When he felt tired he would stand up and go to the sink and get a drink. We then addressed his being prepared. We started with having him bring a pen/pencil and paper. Once he brought his materials, we progressed to having him use the materials. So, I expected him to use the pen and paper to take notes. All the while, I was using the Redirect Behavior Model to help him understand his choices and the impact of each decision. Eventually, with continued conversations and the progression of raising the expectations, he was able to self-regulate his actions with a simple word prompt, such as "materials," "let's get started," or

"what's a better choice?" The use of RBM, PBEs, and conversations helped the student to be more aware of his actions and the impact they would make upon himself.

Andrew Ciochetto,
middle level science

All of the CALM Management techniques that have been presented so far have been leading up to the ultimate goal of developing the students to be responsible citizens, good decision makers, and independent thinkers. The Redirect Behavior Model supports the students through a series of prompts and choices that will give them opportunities to make better choices. Reminding students that for every action there is an equal and opposite reaction, and indicating to students the potential outcomes to their choice(s), will allow them to make an informed decision regarding their choice(s). The Positive Behavior Expectations offer the student a guide for respectful actions and a rationale to address the why for each behavior. CALM Management provides the foundation for students to hold themselves accountable by self-regulating their behaviors and actions. It's a process that requires patience and follow-through. As the student progresses, the expectations will increase and challenge the student eventually to be in control of their own behavior and learning environment. The CALM Management system is based on developing the students' awareness of their actions, holding them accountable for their actions. In doing so, they are making better choices.

This chapter will explore how to establish norms for small-group collaboration. Accountability is essential in being able to trust your students to work as a team and meet the objective of the lesson. Small-group collaboration can have a positive impact on student outcomes. It provides an opportunity for students to explain concepts with their peers and to explore new ideas; furthermore, it empowers students to be able to provide feedback and assess their learning, both individually and in a small-group environment.

While the potential for collaborative work groups is substantial, it is not always guaranteed that learning targets will be met by all the team members. Establishing collaborative small-group norms is essential to the success of the learning outcomes.

Think Beyond the Four Walls . . .

Now the fun can begin. We are able to engage the students in the content on a much higher level—a level in which students are asking questions pertaining to knowledge, comprehension, synthesis, and analysis. I place a high value on teamwork, problem-solving, and engaging students in authentic experiences. Project-based learning offers students an opportunity to explore innovative techniques to put theory into action—to be creative in their thinking when presented with challenges. Inspire students to implement innovative techniques to solve problems, to go on a journey of self-discovery and inquiry-based learning. The diversity of the team can produce inventive approaches to process through a dilemma. Having students employ the concepts learned in class instead of listening to a lecture and taking notes will have a long-lasting impact on their growth and learning.

I challenge you to think beyond the four walls. If there is a problem or challenge that presents itself during a lesson, get excited! This is when you begin to think beyond the four walls. Go beyond the boundaries, take a risk, and be resourceful in teaching your content. Have fun! Yes, you are allowed! Have fun and use your imagination. Create new spaces in your classroom. Go outside. Explore. Take the students to the next level of involvement. Your students will be happier, and I guarantee you will be happier as well.

Quick Wins

Novice teachers: When thinking about the Small-Group Interaction Model, concentrate on just a few of the components. Focus on matching the activity to the objective, materials needed, having clear and concise directions before you place students into their groups. As you progress, you may begin to use more creative methods for the activity and assessment.

Small-Group Interaction Model

When do I give directions, before or after I get my students into groups? When do I hand out materials? What prompts students to move to the next station? Where should all of the materials be placed? What should the groups do if they finish early? Or not finish at all?

These were often questions students asked in my undergraduate courses. They were great questions, and just as I had with all of my proactive measures, I did a task analysis and began to map an outline for teachers to follow. It's a flowchart (see Figure 5.1) that outlines items teachers need to address and prepare prior to the activity. It also serves as a reminder of items for teachers to address. So often we forget about the little items, such as materials, or where to hand in finished products.

The Small-Group Interaction Model provides a structure for teachers to consider before they engage students in a small-group activity. It is a preventative method so students are able to engage in a culture of cooperation. The Voice-Movement-Task Model can easily be incorporated into this model for the pre-teaching of expectations prior to an activity. The Small-Group Interaction Model takes it a step further in preparing the teacher and students for the activity.

> Use an attention-getter liberally to refocus student attention. Do not talk above student voices.

Prior to Activity (Standard Procedures for All Activities)

These are items you may consider prior to every activity. Some of the items you may mention while reviewing VMT. Listed are the items to consider prior to the activity:

- Objective

  What is the purpose of the activity? How will this activity address the student learning outcomes? How will you assess student progress?

The assessment will need to meet the objective. The activity must focus on the element that will inform your teaching according to the assessment feedback.

- Grouping strategies

  Be creative. Challenge yourself to go beyond having students number off, 1–4. There are plenty of unique grouping strategies available online.

- Student roles

  Designate students for particular roles, or randomly assign students a role within their small group. Roles may include: Leader, Recorder, Checker, Presenter, Timekeeper, Summarizer, or Reflector.

- Group size

  Match the group size with the activity. The ideal group size is comprised of three or four students. Often, beyond four members will tend to find it difficult to maintain a high level of participation.

- Physical setup of the classroom

  This will be addressed during the Movement/Materials portion of VMT.

  Consider the optimal design for the seating arrangement. Will students sit on the floor? In a circle? In pods? Reserve time for students to arrange the desks or tables for the activity.

- Materials

  This will be addressed during the Movement/Materials portion of VMT.

When Dr. Lentfer introduced the Small-Group Interaction Model it answered a lot of questions. I wasn't always sure when to give directions. Should I give directions when students were in their groups or before I placed them in their groups? The model was a road map for me to follow when I was planning for instruction. They were great reminders when we were doing collaborative work groups.

Michael Stennis,
pre-service elementary

Address where the materials will be located. Indicate what students should do with the access materials. And finally, communicate the expectation of cleaning their work area before the end of class. Communicate the expectation, practice the expectation, and follow through with the expectation of how to handle the materials.

- Duration

How long will this activity take for students to complete their assigned work? Communicate the timed expectation to the students. Prompt students throughout the activity regarding how much time they have left. Let them know what they should have completed by a certain point.

- Check work

Consider having the answers available in a binder for students to check their answers.

You may have the binder with answers or the binder may be located in a designated area, but have students correct their work according to the answers.

- Final product

The final product can be in multiple forms—video recording, presentations, posters, essay, commercial, or songs. Have a clear vision as to the expectations for the final product. Once you have the essential components, create a rubric that reflects your assessment expectations.

- Communication

The Voice-Movement-Task Model is very helpful for collaborative work group activities. Adjust the components to meet the needs of your students. For example, Voice may address implementing the Student Communication Model (SCM) as students discuss potential solutions; Movement may address how students will move desks for their groups; and Task may implement Option 2 for directions (see page 107 for Option 2).

FIGURE 5.1   Small-Group Interaction Model

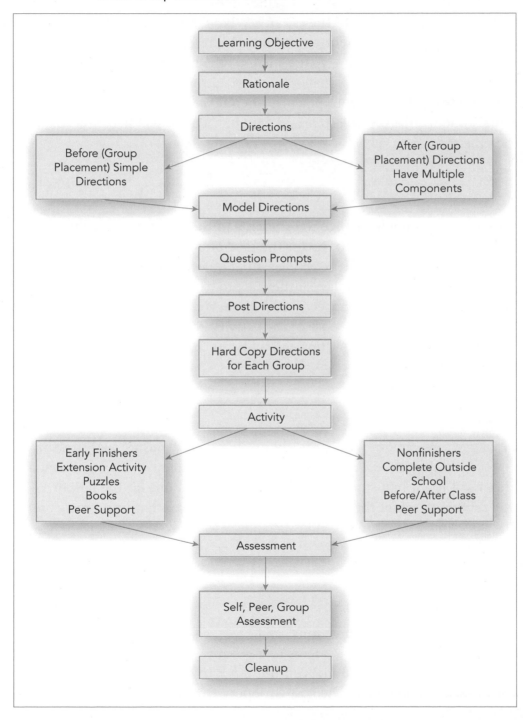

Learning Objectives

Make clear the objectives of the activity. What is the desired end result? It does not take long to mention and have it posted for students to view. The learning outcome will give the students the big picture of what is to be expected regarding the collaborative work group activity. The learning outcome will also guide your practice when reviewing how you will assess if the students met the objective and why the activity will help you to meet the objective.

Rationale

Why are you going to engage the students in the small-group activity? Are you going to do an activity for the sake of doing an activity? How is the activity going to further the learning objective? Group work should address more complex, authentic problems for students to solve, incorporating multiple perspectives from each group member. The rationale addresses the purpose of the activity. Stating the rationale will communicate clear expectations and make students aware of the why of the activity.

Directions/Task

Once you have followed the protocol in Chapter 4 to ensure that students understand the directions and steps needed to complete the task, it is then important to prompt students to consider the directions for the task in a way that will prompt them to ask questions about content (not procedure). The directions should be given in such a way as to promote independent thinking.

When to Give Directions

Prior to Grouping: If directions can be relayed in 3–5 directives, give them prior to forming the students into groups. And continue through the Small-Group Interaction Model continuum. If the directions require more than 3–5 steps, proceed to the Post-Grouping Options.

Post-Grouping Options: Give the directions for the activity after students are formed in their groups. If the directions are complex and lengthy, there are a couple of options:

- *Option 1:* Consider giving a few directions prior to getting students into groups and finish the directions after the groups are formed. Also, review your directions and delete any extra wording. Get to the point. The adage of "less is more" comes into play here.

- *Option 2:* Get the students into their groups and give the directions after they have settled. Do not begin giving directions until you have the attention of all students before you. This is one of the drawbacks to presenting directions after students are in their groups—they tend to become unsettled and talkative. This strategy can work, but it is useful only if you follow through on commanding everyone's attention before you move to the directions.

A strategy that works for me is to embrace the chaos. Take a moment to have the students acknowledge their teammates and tell them, "Thank you for being a part of our team." Many do so with a fist bump or high five. It takes a minute to embrace the novelty of new teammates. This is a proactive strategy that manages time and provides a positive beginning for the new group of students.

Quick Wins

Keep this simple. If you give the directions before or after students are in their groups, you need to use an attention-getter to resume their attention. Wait until all are focused and ready to listen before you proceed with your directions. Do not talk above the student voices. Once you demand their attention by waiting, the next time will not take as long to get their full attention.

- Model the activity

  Simply listing off the directions will not be sufficient to ensure the students will know exactly what is expected. Model the activity. This should take no more than 2 minutes. Have your materials prepared prior to the activity. Use an example that is easy for students to follow.

Consider using an example that may not be content related. For example, if you are reviewing an excerpt from *Romeo and Juliet,* try using an excerpt from a current event or a pop culture item as an example.

- Have students model the activity

  Invite students to model the activity. This is an add-on from the previous "model the activity."

- Question prompts

  Use question prompts to check for understanding. Keep the pace with rapid questions regarding the directions. Random questioning as a whole-group strategy will keep the timing on track.

- Students restate the directions

  This supports students in allowing them to take responsibility to listen to and comprehend the expectations of the group activity. It especially benefits English language learners.

Activity

Students will engage in the activity within their cooperative learning groups. As the teacher, your role is to facilitate the activity and ensure the students are actively engaged and working cooperatively with one another.

Assessment

Assessing group work uses the same principles for assessing individual work. Depending on the learning objective, the teacher may consider assessing the final product, process, and collaborative efforts. Rubrics convey expectations in a clear and concise manner.

Early Finishers

This is an important component for management and instruction. If students finish early, have a plan in place in which they may participate. Consider extension activities, articles, puzzles, organizing class materials, and peer support for nonfinishers.

Nonfinishers

Some groups may not finish within the allotted time. Continue to prompt the group throughout the activity regarding the time. This group may need question prompts to generate a more efficient work level. Groups may have to work on their own time outside of class, or they may work in your classroom before or after school. Consider having students who finish early help struggling groups. The expectation for peer support is to use questions to prompt students to complete their tasks. The peer support students should not finish the work for students outside their group. They are simply there to provide support. If the group has questions, the peer support may guide the students to find the answer, prompt them to focus on completing tasks, or delegate tasks for all students in the group to be more efficient in completing the project.

> Always have a plan for the early finishers—ongoing projects, extension activities, peer support.

Cleanup

Cleanup may appear to be of low importance. Why should this be expected? Students won't want to clean up. Is this battle worth fighting? If you place an expectation and follow through with the expectation, students will follow your directive. Don't dismiss the small things. Having students participate in cleaning up at the end of class provides multiple benefits for you and the students.

It builds upon creating that culture of pride in community. Students are responsible for keeping their classroom community clean and clear of clutter. If you have 30 students, you have 30 workers. You should not be doing the work. If a student has a content question, is it best practice to solve it for them? No, you use question prompts to guide the student to answer their own question. Taking time to clean up shares this same philosophy. Should you be responsible and clean the room after the students have finished their project? Should students be standing around talking, waiting for the bell to ring while you frantically run around the room, trying to clean and organize before the next class enters? No—have the students clean and take pride in their work and their work environment.

> Discipline is in the details; it establishes a culture of pride and respect. Have students clean and maintain their learning environment.

Having the expectation and providing time for students to actively clean their area will allow the teacher to concentrate on content. The teacher will be able to evaluate or make suggestions regarding finished products. Reserve time for the students to clean and organize the room. Instill the high expectation of students cleaning their work area and follow through with this expectation. Do not release the students until the room is up to your standards. Use this strategy in the beginning; students will improve with time and follow through on your part. It will only take a few times for students to understand you mean business if you do not release them until the room is clean and organized.

> When you first introduce a group activity involving stations, try using topics that relate to the students (sports, music, video games). The idea is to train students on the expectations of the activity—rotation directions, on-topic conversations, hand in materials, cleanup, etc.

A CALM classroom will allow the teacher to empower students within collaborative work groups. By implementing the CALM proactive methods and using the Small-Group Interaction Model as a guide, the teacher will be able to teach students how to properly give and receive feedback with a collaborative work group setting.

Peer Feedback

The idea behind developing collaborative work groups is to promote and encourage student voice and empower students by enabling them to be in control of their learning environment. The next step in collaborative work groups is to teach students to give/receive peer feedback. Peer feedback enhances student learning. Students learn from others' mistakes and successes. When students provide academic feedback, they develop a deeper understanding of the content. By working with a set of criteria, students are able to hold each other accountable for their work.

Teachers may hesitate to allow students to peer assess; this is often due to a lack of trust. Teachers may not trust the students are providing effective feedback. It is important to take the time to teach students *how* to give feedback, instead of assuming students know how to give supportive feedback. By taking the time to teach students to peer assess, the teacher will be enabled to trust the students to provide proficient feedback.

How to Teach Students to Provide Academic Feedback

Actively engaging students in the assessment process can have a positive impact on student achievement. It is essential that you make the assessment criteria clear and concise. Keep the process simple. Trust is an absolute key to success. A teacher has to be able to trust the students to give feedback in an appropriate manner. Teach the students how to give feedback, and once they have learned how, trust that they will do it well.

1. Share the Learning Objective

    The learning objective of the lesson should answer the question, "What are we learning, and why?" Share the learning objective for the collaborative learning group activity with the students and match the assessment with the objective.

2. Create Success Criteria

    Success criteria answer the question, "How will we know when we've obtained the learning objective?" Shift the ownership of learning by empowering students in creating the success criteria. Students will begin to foster a deeper commitment to the learning objective when they are involved in the process of creating the assessment instrument. For further information that addresses learning objectives and success criteria, you could read *Challenging Learning Through Feedback,* by James Nottingham.

3. Use Peer Assessments as Formative Assessments

Peer assessment is a method of assessment that can inform your teaching and be helpful in gauging individual contributions during collaborative work group efforts. Based on the results of the peer assessments, you can make adjustments in areas you need to cover again or reemphasize.

4. Learn From Mistakes

Have fun. Take a risk. Engage students in the process as much as possible. It may not look and sound like you want it the first time, but understand that it's a process. It is not going to be perfect the first time. Reflect on the process and adjust your teaching accordingly. If most of the students had trouble in one particular area, reflect and change your method of communicating that learning objective.

Before we went out for our practicum, Dr. Lentfer taught us how to give and receive feedback from our peers. We had a peer support system where we observed and gave one another feedback regarding our delivery of a lesson. She had us role-play and practice before we went out to the field. It helped us, so I taught the same method to my high school students. They were peer editing. It helped to calm the classroom.

Nicholas Hoff,
pre-service middle school math

5. Use Your Extra Time for Support and Enrichment

By taking the time to teach students how to give and receive feedback, you will have more time to address students who need extra support or extension activities. Thirty students = 30 workers. Put them to work, develop a sense of student ownership. Students love to feel important. What a wonderful opportunity to let them feel like they are the teachers.

What Does Feedback Look and Sound Like?

The person giving feedback should do so with a sense of understanding, yet be able to get to the point with direct intent. The person receiving the feedback should leave the conversation with a new goal to concentrate their efforts and a sense of accomplishment. Feedback is not to condemn, but to correct. It is a method to improve performance, not to demean a person.

Students should have a calm demeanor. Voice tone should be caring. Students should face one another in an open-conversation position, with one person talking at a time. The student receiving the feedback needs to be able to listen without interruption and accept feedback. If a student does not agree with the feedback, the student will have a chance to address any issues when they are developing a plan of action. Feedback is not designed for a one-way method of communication. Peer feedback is a respectful sharing of ideas with the ultimate goal of developing progression of growth and learning.

> Take the time to teach students how to properly give and receive feedback. This will build trust, and the teacher will be more willing to employ peer feedback throughout the semester.

Positive Behavior Expectations for Feedback

Give Feedback

- Observe the event.
- Write down positive attributes.
- Write down suggestions for improvement.
- Make sure all comments are supportive.
- Thank the person(s) for their efforts.

Rationale: Your peers will learn and grow from your feedback.

Receive Feedback

- Listen to or read the feedback.

- Think about how the feedback can improve your skills.

- Think about how you may incorporate the feedback.

- Thank them for their feedback.

Rationale: Feedback is always an opportunity to become a better student.

Develop a Plan of Action After Feedback

- One person talks at a time.

- Offer suggestions.

- Listen to suggestions.

- Coconstruct a plan that addresses the area of challenge.

- Agree upon the plan.

- Thank the person(s) for their time and suggestions.

Rationale: Coconstructing a plan will enable the students to identify a learning objective and be able to hold one another accountable for their plan of action.

Implement Feedback

- Think about the feedback you received.

- Construct a goal as to when and how you are going to implement feedback.

- Organize and plan any materials needed to implement feedback.

- Implement the plan that addresses the goal.

- Revisit the goal to check if you achieved your goal.

- Ask for more feedback if necessary.

Rationale: It's important to be able to accept the feedback and follow through with the suggestions to enhance your growth as a student and person.

Role-Play Scenarios

Students need time to practice giving feedback. The best time to teach giving feedback is early in the semester. Have students role-play scenarios. Try creating scenarios that relate to the students. This makes it interesting and fun to learn feedback methods. Start small with the criteria, use a checklist, and progress from a checklist to a rubric.

This way students can evaluate another student's work and identify corrective teaching areas, and together students will develop a plan of action that addresses the area of challenge. Finally, each participant will thank the other for their time and feedback. Have the students follow the PBEs that address feedback.

The more the students practice, the better they will become at identifying areas of challenge. They will begin to feel more comfortable in delivering the message. Eventually, they will not need the steps that address feedback. It will become a part of their vernacular, and it will sound much more like a conversation—a conversation that is supportive and has the best interest of each participant. The same is true for all the Positive Behavior Expectations (PBEs), the Student Communication Model (SCM), and the Redirect Behavior Model (RBM). The more you practice, the more your confidence will increase, and the more it will sound conversational. Stay with it, and the conversations will improve.

One of the benefits of students learning how to provide peer feedback is that they will gradually want—at times, demand—more feedback and better feedback. Feedback plays a large part of classroom culture—a culture of support, team effort, and willingness to improve. If you are consistent in setting the expectations for behavior and academics, students will meet and exceed expectations. Together, you and your students will build a culture of support, and students will increasingly be eager to improve their performance.

Summary

Efficient collaborative work groups enable the teacher and students to dig deeper into the content. Management and instruction coexist to foster a supportive, trusting culture in which students are able to hold one another accountable with their behavior and academics.

Reflection Questions

- How does the Small-Group Interaction Model help to guide your instruction? Does it assist in lesson planning? Does it help in planning for all the details a teacher may not consider prior to a lesson?

- Do you hesitate to utilize peer feedback in your classroom? Do you trust the students to give meaningful or appropriate feedback?

- How does peer feedback impact student achievement? Will taking the time to teach the students how to give/receive feedback increase your trust in their ability to give feedback appropriately?

- If you use peer feedback in your classroom, do you think it is beneficial for students to be able to articulate feedback for their peers?

Quick Wins

- Have students record themselves to evaluate themselves giving feedback.

- Have students maintain goals and revisit their goals throughout each collaborative group activity.

- Pinpoint exactly what you want to evaluate. Consider having students evaluate one academic and one behavior objective. Gradually increase the number of objectives to be assessed.

6

Accountability—
Choices, Consequences,
and Follow Through

For many years I employed the basic consequence that all teachers would use for students who displayed repetitive disruptive behavior—detentions, removal from class, and sending them to the administrator. All of these methods were standard among educators. But I questioned how much the student was learning how to behave appropriately when I sent them out of the room. Did the consequence address the behavior? Did the consequence diminish the inappropriate behavior? The answer was "sometimes." Some students' removal from class and a phone call home would take care of the situation. But there was always a student for whom the basic classroom management techniques did nothing to deter their behavior. In these cases, it would heighten the occurrence of disruption after the consequence. I felt that the detention or removal from class would further the divide between myself and the student. I sensed that I wouldn't be able to get them back into my class in a philosophical sense. I reconsidered my method of using consequences with these students.

I knew I had to develop the relationship, yet hold them accountable for their behavior. Instead of viewing a detention as a negative consequence, I used it more as an opportunity to teach how to make better choices. I was going to use conversations as a resource.

One summer I decided to try something different with my repeat offenders. I decided I would have the students come in for lunch detentions to talk. Conversations were going to be my strategy, and for some that was an unpleasant consequence. The last thing they wanted to do was to spend more time with the lady who droned on about their behavior. Although the repeat offenders seemed exasperated by these talks at the time, to my surprise I've had students come back to me years later to thank me for the time I spent with them having those lunch conversations.

One particular student, Thomas, was having trouble following most of our Positive Behavior Expectations. He and I had numerous lunch conversations, and eventually he understood the importance of how his actions affected him and his peers. Thomas was having trouble making the connection between his actions and how those actions not only had consequences but revealed how he truly viewed himself. He had a negative image of himself. It was difficult for him to imagine himself beyond the gangs on the streets. He was angry and frustrated, and took it out on other students. He could have been viewed as a bully. During our conversations, Thomas revealed that he had a big heart; he just didn't know how to control his anger at times. Thomas made improvements throughout the year, but still had difficulty with his behavior.

Several years later, he found his way back to my room. He told me a story of how he used what he learned from our conversations to stand up to a guy who was making fun of a student who was struggling in class with taking tests. He held onto these words: "Thomas, your actions have a reaction. It can be a positive or negative reaction, but just remember that your words and actions are never about the other person, they are always how you feel about yourself. If you cut down another student for failing a test, that tells me there is something about that student you see in yourself. When you criticize, it's never about that person—it's always about how you feel about yourself." It was through these many conversations in middle school that he remembered those words throughout high school. He said that when he would want to criticize someone, he would always stop and reflect what it was about that person that bothered him about himself and then he would try to change that aspect of himself for the better. Thomas thanked me and even apologized for his actions in class. I told him that it had all worked out for the best because if he hadn't misbehaved in my class, we wouldn't have had the opportunity to have our lunch conversations, and it could have taken him years to learn about behavior, decisions, and consequences.

It confirmed to me that taking the time to have a conversation instead of kicking a student out of class has a powerful effect on student outcomes. You may not see the results right away, but the time you offer the student can have a positive influence on their life—which is tremendously rewarding!

Student Choices

If you think about it, you can't make anyone do anything they do not want to do. I can't make a student take notes if they don't want to. I can't make students turn in their homework, present their results, or share their materials if they do not want to.

So, how do you get someone to do something they may not want to do? You can give them all the information they need, educate them on the impact of their choice, and let them make an educated decision. What better way to develop students to become better decision makers, responsible citizens, and hold them accountable for their decisions than to present all of their choices? I decided to let the students be in charge of their learning and truly empowered them by giving them choices. I maintained the mantra of "Do the Right Thing: Make Good Choices."

Once I began to give my students choices, it reduced the occurrence of arguing considerably. Not only did arguing diminish, but it allowed the students to learn how their choices impacted themselves and other people in their lives.

Examples:

Student Choice	Consequence
Won't listen during instructions	Proximity, RBM Phase I or II, Outside of Class Conversation

(Continued)

(Continued)

Student Choice	Consequence
Won't take notes	Proximity, RBM Phase I or II, Outside of Class Conversation
Talks to peers during class	Proximity, RBM Phase I or II, Outside of Class Conversation
Doesn't do class work	RBM Phase I or II, Outside of Class Conversation
Argues with teacher/is disrespectful	RBM Phase I or III, Outside of Class Conversation

Once you have established the potential consequences with the class, the students are then able to make an informed decision regarding their behavior. Again, the choices depend on the level of disruption, the number of previous interactions with the students, and the phase of the Redirect Behavior Model (RBM).

Let's review how RBM provides choices for the student. The teacher will redirect the student using either Phase I or Phase II. If, after the initial redirection, the student resumes the behavior initially displayed, the teacher will go over to the student and present them with choices. If the student is not escalating and is open to receiving more information regarding their choices, the teacher will go over in-depth the impact and rationale of the possible choices upon which the student has to decide. After stating the choices, the teacher will give the student time to think about their choices.

General education teachers will have students with behavior disorders, and teachers lack the ability to effectively implement strategies to diffuse potentially volatile situations (Kaff, Zabel, & Milham, 2007; Niesyn, 2009). More specifically, teachers lack the knowledge and skills of how to redirect behavior (Niesyn, 2009; Westling, 2010). Managing behavior is a predominant element of stress for novice teachers, and it is difficult to master (Corbell, Booth, & Reiman, 2010). Generally, pre-service teachers are taught minimal behavior strategies (Tillery, Varjas, Meyers, & Collins, 2009), but they often rely on future training when they receive their first teaching position (Sugai, Horner, & McIntosh, 2008).

In the Social Cognitive Theory, Bandura (1986) contends that learning occurs in a social context through the following constructs: social interaction (teacher/student efficacy), cognitive environment (values and character), and behavior (engagement). Bandura (1997) suggests there is a constant interaction and causation between behavior and human cognition and the environment. It concentrates on the social influences, with the emphasis on internal and external social influences. Students learn social skills via interactions and observations with other students and teachers (Schunk & Usher, 2013). Having alternative proactive strategies is necessary for teachers of all levels and content areas. Providing students with academic choices can transfer to behaviors as well. Presenting students with choices will empower them to be in control of their behavior. Let's take a closer look at how choices can be provided for behavior.

> *Implementing the CALM Classroom Process highlighted the need to use conversations as a consequence. I knew that developing positive relationships is a key to successfully manage a classroom. I had a student I had been working with throughout the semester. I continually gave him detentions after school for a consequence. When Dr. Lentfer began to ask me questions about the students' interests, home life, and study skills, I didn't have an answer for a lot of her questions. In fact, I kept thinking, "Why is Dr. Lentfer asking me these questions when all I want to know is what to do with this student?" My student wouldn't follow any of my directions, wouldn't complete or even start his work every day. I was frustrated. But it also became very clear to me that I knew little to nothing about my student.*
>
> *Dr. Lentfer suggested I take the time to have a conversation during the detention. I was skeptical, but decided to try it. I was amazed at what I didn't know about my student. He wasn't completing his work because he was going to work in the evenings and wouldn't get home until midnight some nights. That explained his low motivation and always wanting to sleep in my class. He also had to get up early to get his three younger siblings ready for school because his parents were at work early in the mornings. This explained why he didn't have time to complete his homework. As soon as I took the time to have conversations with this student, we began to come up with a plan to get him caught up on his work, and his attitude changed. Because I took the time*
>
> *(Continued)*

(Continued)

to get to know him and worked with him and his situation, his attitude and work ethic changed. I have since implemented the CALM Classroom Process and used conversations explicitly as a consequence. I say "consequence," which has a negative connotation, but it always ended up to be a positive experience with my students. It doesn't take long to have those conversations. I rely so heavily on conversations because I know the conversations will eventually work. I now use conversations as a tool to develop relationships and improve student effort.

Daniel Stokes,
science, Grades 7–12

Providing students with choices allows them to be accountable for their actions, with the assistance of the teacher to follow through on holding them accountable through positive and negative consequences. By giving students choices, they learn to be responsible and learn life lessons. They are less likely to make excuses, argue with the teacher, and blame other students for their behavior when they are held accountable for the decisions they make in the classroom. Student choice will get students to invest in themselves. Give the students choices and follow through with the consequences; they are then able to see the impact of their decisions. This can be powerful and lead the students to invest in themselves with a more critical viewpoint. Students need to understand that they will be held accountable for their actions.

Organizing the structure of the classroom in a way that provides students with choice and accountability can be a balancing act for teachers. The biggest fear teachers envision is the possibility of the classroom getting out of control (Alderman, 2008). We revisit the idea of relationships and how well you know your students. You will know the amount of autonomy you may afford each student. If you have your consequences prepared prior to the beginning of the year, this will provide a sound framework. The overall approach is to communicate the specific behaviors, rationale, and the consequences if not demonstrated properly. It is through this framework that you will begin to establish a culture of accountability and responsibility toward self and others. This will foster a supportive classroom community.

Consequences to Promote Growth

A Shift in Thinking

How often have you heard or used these phrases: *If you don't stop talking and begin taking notes, you are going to have to stay after school!* or, *If you don't sit down and begin your classwork, you are going to have extra homework!* The homework threat is always humorous to me. If the student is repeatedly off task, I can almost guarantee the warning of after-school detention or extra homework will not be a deterrent, especially when you deliver the consequence as a threat.

I am sure some of you are thinking that these phrases aren't "threats" but simply consequences for what happens when classwork is not completed. Of course, there need to be consequences when a student doesn't do what is asked. However, when you are dealing with a student who is noncompliant and has already been detained after school numerous times for not doing homework, they are going to perceive your consequence as another threat. Very likely, they will react by becoming defensive or shutting down. Either way, the consequence is not effective. Consequences presented as threats are counterproductive and reactive; they do not teach students how to correct their behavior. To be effective, consequences have to have meaning and relevance with the student, and fit the level of disruption. I challenge you to think about consequences through a more positive and educational lens. Remember, your goal is to teach both behavior and the academic curriculum.

Place your energy on positive consequences, even during the times when you feel you have zero positive energy left. Dig deep and substitute negative consequences with supportive value statements that nurture students. Telling your students that they are valued and treasured members of the classroom community will have a powerfully positive impact on their behavior. Think about how you feel when someone values you as a person and explicitly states that they enjoy having you around. Being valued and feeling wanted makes you feel good. If you let students know you value them and want them to succeed, they will want to stay in your classroom.

How can a consequence be positive? Begin by teaching students that for every choice, there is a consequence. When teaching students about their choices, tell them how every action has a reaction, and the reaction could be positive or negative. So, if a student is quiet and takes notes during instruction, they will be able to successfully complete their assignment, therefore increasing their chances of receiving a favorable grade. This can be viewed as a positive action and will result in a positive reaction. This may seem like obvious logic, but many students do not yet have the maturity level fully to comprehend these logical consequences.

For example, instead of offering a consequence that may be seen as a punishment, provide a consequence that will lead to the student's growth and improvement. If a student is being disruptive or is off task, designate a time to have a conversation with the student to develop a plan of action to modify their behavior. Have them discuss with you a rationale as to why it's important to have positive behavior: How does that positive behavior affect their academic and social life? How does that behavior affect their friends, teachers, and family? Help them make the connections between their choices and the logical consequences of those choices. Use questioning prompts to empower them to develop a rationale for staying on task and to help them decide on the adjustments they will need to make to stay on task in the future.

> *I began to consider positive consequences. By giving students choices and positive reinforcement, I believe this will assist in promoting positive behavior.*
>
> Nataly Orozco,
> middle level math/science

Activity

When you are discussing the PBEs, invite students to come up with positive consequences. Have them also draft the rationale explaining why the consequence matches the disruption. The frequency of the disruption should also play a part in the progression of consequences. Guide students via prompting questions.

They can create posters with statements and pictures to post on the walls. They can also record themselves describing the consequences and rationale. These activities establish a solid foundation for a cooperative, safe classroom community.

Conversations to Promote Growth

I encourage you to have many conversations with your students. Talk to them about their goals, their ideas, and their struggles. Disruptive behavior shouldn't be the only prompt to have a conversation. The conversations don't have to be long; just begin to get to know your students. A 2-minute conversation can cover quite a bit of ground.

Anytime you involve students in the process of creating the classroom expectations and consequences, it makes it much easier for the teacher, especially a new teacher, to hold the students accountable. They can't argue much if they were a part of creating the expectations and consequences.

Chris Jackson,
pre-service physics

I especially loved lunch conversations with my students. Time was limited, but it allowed us to focus our conversation—and we would eat, which created more of a relaxed environment. I would be very intentional when starting the conversation. I would indicate the specifics of why we were having a conversation. I would review the misbehavior and indicate what I needed the student to display and follow with value statements. So, in effect, I would use RBM, Phase I. But I would always ask, *What's going on? What is keeping you from being able to display the appropriate behavior? How can I help you be successful?* The main goal is to provide a space for the student to talk; your job is to listen and ask prompting questions. Together, you agree upon an action strategy to improve the student's behavior.

Approaching consequences also needs to be logical and natural:

Natural consequences are based on the result of the misbehavior. Example: If you are not on task during independent work time, you will have to complete the assignment outside of class.

Logical consequences are the consequences upon which teacher and student agree. Example: The class agreed to have no running during a class activity, but student A runs to get a crayon and on the way knocks student B's project off the table. Student B screams and gets upset. The teacher needs to approach the situation by letting both students know that everyone is upset right now, and that she is going to talk to student A and come back to student B in a moment. The teacher will need to use Phase II of RBM: What did you do? Why did you do that? What should you have been doing? Ask the student to apologize and help clean up.

How to Approach an Upset Student

How do you feel when you are angry? Do you want to have someone talk to you about your part in the situation? Do you like to have someone tell you what you did wrong? No! No one likes anyone to talk to them when they are angry. So, if you do not like it, do not do this with your students. Don't poke the bear. Do not have a conversation with a student when they are upset or close to getting out of control. Give them time and space to calm themselves.

How do you approach a student who is visibly upset? You say to them, "I see you're upset. Why don't you take a moment to gather yourself?" And then walk away. Give them room to calm down. Do not have a conversation with someone who is upset. Let them know you want to talk with them after they have gathered their thoughts.

Once they have calmed down, then you can have that conversation. Try not to forget it or shrug it off. If you feel that the student self-corrected and realizes their responsibility

Dr. Lentfer had us thinking about consequences as more of an opportunity. I always thought consequences were sending a student out of the room. But she had us begin to have quick conversations with the students. I tried it during my practicum, and it worked. A student pushed papers off another student's desk, and I used the Redirect Behavior Model to address the situation. I wasn't even their real classroom teacher, and the students responded to the logical consequence.

Ben Carder,
middle level math

without the conversation, then praise them and let them know they did a great job of self-correcting their behavior.

Relying on Positive Consequences May Require a Change in Mindset

You will always find what you are looking for—it's a mindset. Your mind is a powerful thing. Your thoughts become actions, and your actions have an impact on you and the people around you. The impact can be positive or negative—you choose.

If you think that a student will be difficult, you will always perceive that student as being difficult. If you have had conversations with the student and developed goals that address their behavior, believe in the process. It takes time, but you have to give the student a chance to succeed and a chance to make mistakes. If they make a mistake, teach them by using Phase II of RBM. Use questioning prompts to guide them to a solution and a rationale. The ultimate goal is to have the student become an independent thinker and make good choices.

Challenge yourself to adjust your mindset and focus on the learning moment, trusting students with a choice and a voice. Understand they are going to make mistakes. They are going to break the rules. Show respect to the student by following through with the consequence related to their choice. You can't expect students to emerge as critical thinkers if you don't give them a chance to make their own decisions. When you teach students to learn how to ride a bike, do you have them watch you ride a bike? Do you have them take notes and nod their head when you are lecturing them on how to properly ride their bike? No. You give them training wheels (Phase I), let them get a feel for the bike, and eventually remove the supports and let them ride on two wheels (Phase II). Hold them accountable to their behavior. Gradually release the decision making to the student.

A shift in thinking can make you feel uncomfortable. This is great! It is precisely when you are feeling uncomfortable while trying to make a positive

I had never thought about consequences as a positive. I always thought consequences were associated with detentions. But when I used positive reinforcements, it helped my students to want to do better, and I was less stressed.

Sarah Bohrer,
middle level language arts

change that growth begins to evolve. Be faithful and persevere through insecure moments. The results are well worth the effort!

Positive Consequences

Positive consequences are actions or supports that reinforce positive behavior. They can be tangible incentives or verbal positive feedback. The idea is to concentrate on celebrating the positive behavior, especially with the students who need a little extra guidance.

A positive consequence is a response to a behavior. Use positive reinforcing language. If you want students to raise their hand to answer a question, remind them to raise their hand to answer or share their answer. For example, a teacher may say, "Can someone raise their hand and describe how . . . ?" After the student shares their response, reinforce their action with a positive comment: "Thank you for raising your hand and sharing your idea."

Concentrate on the positive actions. Request, remind, and reinforce positive behavior with positive word choices from the teacher. Instead of addressing the negative behavior, try consistently to point out the positive behavior displayed in the classroom.

Elementary School

Teacher: *I need all eyes on me. Can I have everyone put their pencils down and eyes on me?* [Students begin to follow instructions.]

Teacher: *José, thank you for following directions and putting your pencil down. Prethy, thank you for quietly placing your pencil down and giving me your attention.*

Middle School/High School

Teacher: *Can someone raise their hand and tell me . . . ?* [Students follow the directions and raise their hand to respond to the teacher.]

Teacher: *Thank you, Ameer, for raising your hand. Go ahead and share your idea.*

Notice how the teacher asked for a specific behavior and praised with positive words identifying the specific behavior.

> *During my practicum, Dr. Lentfer suggested we focus on our word choices. She wanted us to use positive reinforcements to support the appropriate behavior. I began to praise students when they followed directions. It seemed to calm the students and it appeared all the students responded better when I used positive word choices.*
>
> Emma Tuttle,
> elementary grades

> *I recorded several lessons and analyzed student behavior. I noticed a tendency with my students' response to my directions. They were reluctant to follow my directions because I didn't use any positive reinforcements. I would quickly resort to warnings: "If you don't have lower voice tones, you won't be able to work with your partner." Dr. Lentfer suggested I change my word choice. She wanted us to use more praise and positive reinforcements when we saw behavior that was appropriate. I began to praise the students more, and I realized I was calm and the students were more responsive to my directions. The recordings also revealed that the body language, especially of the students who struggled, began to shift. They responded in a more positive way.*
>
> Nataly Orozco,
> middle level math/science

> Positive word choice and positive reinforcements set the tone for a supportive culture. If you concentrate on the negative, the negative will appear. Concentrate on the positive and the positive will flourish.

Consequences That Address Negative Behavior

Negative consequences are used in response to disruptive behavior. They can be used to enforce limits and reinforce rules after simple reminders haven't worked. Carefully consider consequences to make sure they address the behavior and are natural and logical. Overuse of negative consequences can lead to escalation of the situation. Inconsistent use of consequences can have the same effect over time.

Examples of consequences that address negative behavior include:

- General reminder
- Proximity
- Individual reminder
- Seating arrangement
- Warning
- Parent contact
- Partner teacher—complete a behavior improvement plan
- Detention
- Action plan
- Interaction with a team of teachers, administrators, parents
- Action plan according to the team discussion
- Office referral

Inappropriate Responses to Negative Behavior

Negative consequences should not be a contributor to the negative situation. Using RBM will promote a respectful discourse while de-escalating the situation. Negative consequences contribute to the heightening of a volatile situation. Be cautious of using negative consequences as threats. A threat is counterproductive and will result in a negative outcome. If a student hears, "*You better quit talking or I'm going to* _____ [insert consequence]," you know it's not going to end well. It is a threat. Often, the threats are filled with empty promises and leave the student feeling worthless and angry. Choose your words and tone wisely. The Redirect Behavior Model will guide you to begin changing your words to a more positive, supportive phrasing of words.

Examples of negative consequences include:

- Threatening comments

- Vindictive tone and/or comments

- Angry tone

- Gives in to excuses

- Barters with the student

- Condescending tone

Instead of using negative consequences, try implementing a series of supportive value statements. Take time to teach why the behavior is not conducive to the learning environment. Focusing on negative behavior will invoke the highly probable incident that the teacher will see the negative behavior. You will see what you expect to see. For example, if you decide you want a red car—you do not care what kind of car, but you are certain you want a bright red car—you will begin to see every bright red car at every intersection, parking lot, and street. You will manifest your destiny.

Tips for Success

Give students a chance to improve their behavior. Praise them for the smallest of successes and teach to the learning moments that will help them to be successful. It is easy to label students or predict behavior. And at times the prediction may come true, but you have to separate yourself from their behavior and let them make mistakes and correct their mistakes. If you begin to label a student as always off task during instruction, their behavior is heightened in your mind and you will become susceptible to feeling angry and frustrated with that student. Concentrate on the positive moments. Ask the student to tell you what they have done well regarding their behavior. It doesn't always have to come from you. But make sure you are enthusiastic in recognizing their efforts.

Negative Consequences	Consider Trying . . .
Threatening comments "You better stop talking during instruction or you are going to be in after school."	Positive language "John, I understand you may want to talk during instruction, but I need you to stay quiet so you have every chance at being successful. Thank you." Say "thank you" right away; don't give him time to comment. Remember, he likes to talk!
Vindictive, angry, condescending tone and/or comments	Give yourself a timeout. Do not address a student while your emotions are out of control. Take a breath and try one of the following: • Communicate to the student that you are upset and need a moment to gather your thoughts. • You may indicate that you like the student just fine, but you do not like the behavior they are displaying. • Always be honest and let them know that it is not okay to _____ [indicate the unacceptable behavior] and respond in a calm manner.

Negative Consequences	Consider Trying . . .
Barters with student Student tries to barter and the teacher gives in to the student's suggestion. Student has been prompted several times to put away their phone. Student: *"I promise I won't use phone again. I'll put it away."* Teacher agrees and warns not to do it again.	Be assertive while stating their choices and consequences. Offer two choices: (1) the student can self-correct; (2) the student can continue their behavior, but there will be consequences. Assert yourself without any hint of apology in your voice tone. Do not be wishy-washy. Stay away from the following phrases: *I think so, maybe, I'm not sure.* These phrases open the window of opportunity for the student to manipulate a situation. Instead, use definitive phrases: *Yes, you may; No, you will need to; You will need . . .* RBM holds the student accountable.

Quick Wins

Talking during instruction. This is the best place for new teachers to begin. Do not let the students talk while you are talking. Demand silence! And mean it! Talking during instruction can quickly escalate and get out of control. Have an attention-getter and use it! This includes secondary teachers. Wait until students are all quiet before you begin to speak. Demand this early and often. Be consistent and follow through with the wait time. Students will quickly understand and follow your expectation of no talking.

Discipline early and follow through on every expectation, even the smallest of details. Follow through and have the students clean their work space before leaving, have students in their seats working from bell to bell, have students sit up during class, demand that students not talk during instruction. Work hard and have fun. You and the students will have fun if you follow through with the details of discipline.

Consequence Progression

After I began not to take disruptions as a personal attack, I was able to approach behavior in a more objective manner. I began to view disruptions as opportunities to build relationships and guide students to do the right thing: make good choices. I did this by establishing progressive levels of disruption. These levels determined how I would approach the disruption and the potential choices I would present.

Organize your consequences with a progressive sequence of severity. The consequence should match the level of disruption. It is important to note that a particular behavior could potentially be viewed as all three disruption levels. It is dependent on how the student responds and/or how frequently the disruption is displayed.

There are three levels of disruption:

- Level I

  Level I is associated with low-level disruptions: anything that interrupts instruction. These are minor distractions that may impact other students or you as the teacher. They do not require serious consequences. However, if the disruption is not addressed in a timely manner, students may repeat the behavior, and this can lead to more serious consequences. Low-level disruptions can quickly escalate to Level II if you do not address them in a timely and efficient manner. The good news is that this level of behavior can often be redirected with nonverbal prompts such as eye contact, proximity, or a hand motion.

  How you define Level I may depend upon the response of the student. For example, texting may be viewed as Level I or Level II, depending on the response of the student. If you have to address the behavior several times per class, it can fit the description of Level II. If the student follows your instructions and puts the phone away without hesitation, it remains a Level I. Also, if the school or your philosophy regarding cell phones and texting is zero tolerance, you may place texting at Level II.

Here are some examples of Level I disruptions (note that strategies do not necessarily correspond with the levels of disruption):

Level I Disruptions	Strategies for Level I Disruptions
Pen tapping	RBM—Phase I
Texting/passing notes	Wait time—stop instruction
Talking out of turn/ blurting answers	Proximity—move into their space
Chair tipping	Eye contact—teacher look
Chewing gum	Point to poster—PBEs
Arriving late to class	Student name—say their name
Talking quietly during instruction	Quiet quick prompt—1:1 prompt
Poking partner with pen/ pencil	Seating arrangement—move student to an alternative seat
Sleeping	Ask if they feel okay: Do they need to go to the nurse? Offer to get a drink of water.
Not taking notes	Proximity—point or ask if they need materials to take notes.

- Level II

Disruptions may be the same behaviors as Level I disruptions, but may be categorized as more disruptive if the student does not accept the redirection or repeats the disruption with a high-frequency rate.

Level II Disruptions	Strategies for Level II Disruptions
Talking with a neighbor in a *loud* voice during instruction	RBM Phase II

(Continued)

(Continued)

Level II Disruptions	Strategies for Level II Disruptions
Shoving peer's materials off desk	Time with a partner teacher/behavior reflection
Talking to another small group outside of the student's assigned small group	Point deduction from motivation plan
Repeated infraction of PBEs	Conversation—lunch, before/after school, hallway, after class dismissal
	Parent contact
	Inform your team teachers
	Meeting with teacher team, student, parent, administrator—develop an action plan

- Level III

Any disruption that is perceived to be unsafe for the student displaying the behavior or the students in the vicinity of the disruption.

Level III Disruptions	Strategies for Level III Disruptions
Shouting across the room during instruction and/or work time	RBM Phase III
Fighting	Contact parent, teacher team, counselor, administrator
Leaving class without permission	Team teacher—revisit action plan
Argument escalating to a potential fight	Referral to administrator (last resort)

Quick Wins

It is helpful to have a guideline for the consequence progression as a reference for the teacher. You may also post the progression for students to reference as well. The progression should be general in nature. For example, you may include the following:

- Reminder

- Reminder with choices

- Seat change

- Partner teacher—student will go into another teacher's classroom to complete a behavior sheet

- Call home

- Lunch/before/after school conversation—this can be implemented at any point

- Meet with team teachers

- Parent/team meeting—develop a behavior plan

- Parent/team meeting—evaluate progress

It didn't take me long to figure out that if I didn't follow through with my consequences, the students would continue their behavior. Not only would they continue their behavior each time I communicated my expectations, they wouldn't take me seriously because they knew there was a pretty good chance I wouldn't follow through. I reflected on my behavior and changed it before their behavior escalated to a point where it would be difficult to gain back their trust and respect. I was honest with them and admitted I wasn't holding them accountable, but that was going to change. There was a new sheriff in town, and I was going to follow through with my consequences. I admit it was sometimes hard for me to follow through because it was easier at the time to let them off the hook, but in the long run it was easier to redirect them when I did follow through because they knew I would hold them accountable.

Jessica Sorrell,
middle school math and science

Follow Through

Finally, if you do not follow through with the consequences, your teaching interactions will result in just words and no change in behavior. You have to be consistent and follow through. Inconsistent follow-through opens the door for students to test you; they will begin to argue or try to bargain their way out of the consequences. You will be vulnerable to manipulation. They won't take you seriously when you try to redirect their behavior. You will gain more respect from the students if you follow through. Also, you will spend a lot of time and energy trying to regain their trust and respect.

While delivering the consequences it is imperative you remain calm. Take the emotion out of the equation. Remember that the behavior is not your behavior. You are not responsible for the behavior; the students are responsible for their behavior. Maintain the idea that it is not you—it is the student who needs to correct the behavior. This should enable you to remain firm and calm while delivering the consequences.

If you require no talking during instruction, you need to hold the student(s) accountable for agreeing to that behavior expectation. The old adage of "if you give them an inch, they'll take a mile" applies here. This is especially true with talking; if you do not address the talking right away it will quickly escalate and become a problem. It is much easier to address the disruption right away than it is to wait until it gets out of control. If you wait too long it will take longer for students to believe you are going to hold them accountable. So, hold them accountable from the beginning, be consistent, and remain calm while communicating their choices and consequences. Ignoring the expectations will gradually escalate the misbehavior throughout the semester and could lead to a serious situation. It is much easier to be firm with your redirection from the beginning.

Summary

Students are going to break the rules. They may do it with or without intention, but nevertheless, it is important to have the goal for them to be able to remain in the classroom. We need to maximize the time students are engaged in the learning environment, and sending students out of the room does not support their academic needs. Have a plan in place for consequences. Consider replacing the consequence with a conversation. Hold the student accountable during that conversation. And follow through with your consequence.

I started to witness all of the CALM Management methods take effect on student behavior. It began with the Positive Behavior Expectations (PBEs), teaching behaviors via the Redirect Behavior Model (RBM), Student Choices, Class Conversations, and preparing the students to interact appropriately with the Voice-Movement-Task Model (VMT) as well. All of these proactive strategies were having a clear impact on student behavior. And the best part of the whole situation was that the students were gradually taking control of their learning environment because we developed the relationships and trust within our classroom culture.

Reflection Questions

- Think about a time when you might have struggled with a student. Did your consequences improve their behavior?

- Have you ever engaged in a redirection with a student who was angry? What was the result? If you had taken a moment to let the student and yourself calm down, could it have been resolved in a more respectful manner?

- Have you found yourself not following through with the consequences? Does the behavior improve?

- Do you find yourself addressing the same behaviors? Are you talking with the student about their behavior? Are the parents involved? Are you following through with the consequences?

Quick Wins

- Have students create a list of consequences.

- Organize the list of consequences by progressive levels of severity (Levels I, II, III).

- Record your class having a discussion about peer feedback of behavior. Have students reflect on conversations they have had with the teacher regarding their own behavior and how that conversation had an impact on their future behavior. Have them reflect on the class consequences for certain behavior and discuss whether or not those consequences are effective or appropriate. This can be done whole class or with individual students. Consider creating an action plan for students to follow to guide their success.

- Record yourself. Do you give praise? Do you follow through with the consequences? Is your delivery of the consequence believable? Condescending?

C
A
L
M

PART III

LEADERSHIP

7

Teacher as a Leader

>> I may not be the most gifted teacher. I may not be the most organized teacher. I may not have the prettiest lesson plans. And I may not be the smartest teacher. But there is one thing I do know: I can outwork anyone, and so can you. I was fortunate to learn this lesson at a very young age. My mom and dad held all of us kids accountable and had us working on the farm—no questions asked. We may have tried to argue child labor laws, which fell upon deaf ears. Although there were times we could not stand working with the pigs, in the end we do have fond memories. We were able to laugh about a lot of things. But mostly it taught us life lessons that no video game or TV show could teach us. It taught us all the intangibles that teachers and parents try to instill in young people—perseverance, determination, work ethic, respect, responsibility, how to complete a task, how to overcome obstacles, etc. These are the things that separate the successful from the not-so-successful. These are the values I tried to show and teach my students as well. And why not? These core values are the foundation for excellence. It is well worth your time to invest in your students as people. Content and behavior can be blended, and the students will excel. Culture and community matter. Take the time to develop a supportive, calm culture in which students are able to work hard for their goals and take pride in their accomplishments.

Leadership is important for a CALM classroom because it ensures the learning process is continuous and the students are actively engaged. So, what does it mean to be a CALM teacher leader? It starts with a calm confidence. A simple belief in oneself. Living each moment with the passion and purpose that drew you to this profession. The quiet knowing that you are following and believing in your passion. Embrace the challenges and successes with gratitude. It's about having a balance of teaching students how to respect one another and implementing quality instruction. It takes time, patience, and persistence, but it is well worth the effort in teaching the whole child.

> Having a balance of management and quality instruction is instrumental in developing as a teacher leader.

Five Effective Practices for a Teacher Leader

A CALM teacher leader will have an understanding of how to listen to differing perspectives, have a relationship with the students based on trust and respect, allow the students' voices to be heard, and build a culture of community within the classroom. All of this can be accomplished by implementing the following effective practices:

- Reflective practice

- Communication

- Presence

- Positive mindset

- Instruction

The teacher's role is to lead these practices. Leadership is often associated with someone in control or with indirect control. There are benefits to both direct and indirect control. In direct instruction, students are given clear learning objectives, an explanation of the material, and time to practice the skills needed for the learning. It tends to have the teacher play a central role in the learning environment. However, with indirect control the teacher will employ multiple learning modalities, which may include project-based learning, problem-solving, and reflective discussion. Indirect control encourages student voice and sharing ideas. The students are allowed to synthesize the material presented and construct their own conclusions through a way that is relevant and experiential for them. They may create presentations, recordings, art projects, etc. The idea is to present the material and have students direct their learning. The two strategies can complement one another and are often used throughout each learning unit.

In your classroom, you need to maintain a balance between direct and indirect guidance. You need a sense of direct control in order to achieve a well-organized and goal-driven classroom, but you also need to maintain a sense of indirect control where students take accountability for their academic and behavior skills and gain a sense of autonomy. By maintaining a healthy balance between the two, you will find that not only the stress in your life, but the stress among the students, between the students, and even between you and your students, will decrease immensely.

Some teachers really struggle with allowing any indirect control in their classroom. If you implement and follow through with the Positive Behavior Expectations (PBEs), Redirect Behavior Model (RBM), Voice-Movement-Task Model (VMT), Student Communication Model (SCM), and the Community Council (CC), all of these methods will help to transition to a healthy balance between direct and indirect classroom control. In order for this to happen, you have to trust the models and the process. It will take time and perseverance in order to attain a high-functioning, well-behaved classroom. Through implementation, the students will be practicing the expectations and the models. This continuous practice and implementation will build trust and develop a strong, supportive, inclusive classroom community for students to achieve in academics and exhibit characteristics representative of respectful interactions within the classroom.

Reflective Practice

Reflective practice is a process that enhances teaching and learning, and is central in developing as a professional. Teachers who engage in frequent reflection will become more aware of their attitudes, beliefs, and practices, which will enhance their growth and improve the support they give to their students. I challenge you to create opportunities for you to develop your reflective practices. Here are some ideas to consider as a reflective practitioner:

- Recording lessons

- Observation

- Reflective journal

- Mentor

- Professional Learning Community (PLC)

Recording Lessons

Recording yourself teaching a lesson can be a powerful tool to use to improve your instruction. When you first begin this practice, you may feel uncomfortable watching yourself; with time and practice this will eventually go away. As you are recording yourself, reflect on your practices as well as your students' interactions. How are the students reacting to your instruction? Word choice? Who are you calling on? What is your response to student interactions? How might your beliefs impact your practices? What are your word choices, movements, nonverbal messages? Continue to analyze all areas of your instruction. Does your classroom reflect your student body? Jim Knight is an expert in the field of coaching and video coaching. His books, webinars, and conferences are wonderful resources to begin the process of analyzing your teaching through video. I especially recommend *Focus on Teaching: Using Video for High-Impact Instruction*.

Observation

It is easy to get caught up in your day-to-day routines throughout the year. I challenge you to take time to visit another teacher's classroom. This offers a different perspective on how to approach your instruction. Observe a peer who teaches the same subject and a teacher in another grade level or subject area outside of your expertise. This may give you alternative approaches to differentiate your instruction. Before the observation, make sure you are prepared. Identify a few areas in which you are interested in improving your skills—focus on behaviors of the students and teacher and their responses, instructional strategies, transitions, literacy strategies, etc. Take notes on the interactions and plan a time to meet with the teacher for reflection. Also, reiterate that you are not there to evaluate their teaching; you are there to learn and grow from their expertise. Finally, invite teachers into your classroom as well. This is a great way to share feedback, successes, and challenges.

Reflective Journal

Keeping a journal can be helpful with your teaching practices and help you sort through areas of challenge and success. Journaling can relieve stress and provide another outlet for reflection. When you write, your words and stream of consciousness can flow and reveal new and innovative insights. I often wrote notes or a short reflection on my lesson plan. Writing my reflection on the lesson plan proved to be an efficient practice because I did not have to try to find my reflection in another location, such as my journal. But I did use a journal as well. I would reflect on lessons in it, but mostly I used it to write stories. This was always a fun activity because it helped relieve stress and helped put things into perspective.

Mentor

Be intentional in choosing a mentor. Trust and respect are key factors in choosing an appropriate mentor. A mentor is not an evaluator, but a confidante. Mentors are especially helpful for new teachers. The novice teacher should be confident the mentor will not judge them for their mistakes and feelings of doubt. A mentor is there to help with areas of challenge, and to encourage and inspire the teacher to improve their practices.

Professional Learning Community

The purpose of the Professional Learning Community (PLC) is to connect with colleagues on a consistent basis to collaborate on action research projects to increase student achievement: an ongoing professional development among colleagues within a school, district, and community. It as an action-oriented group that addresses the current needs of the students. It uses data to identify areas of need. The members will examine multiple factors that may influence the area of need and create new student outcomes. Through this process, they will identify new teaching strategies and prepare teachers to deliver higher-quality instruction.

In addition, this is an opportunity to network with leaders in your school, district, and community. Learn from your network, but challenge yourself to take the lead in an area about which you feel passionately. This will not only showcase your leadership skills, but your colleagues will benefit greatly from your expertise.

Communication

Effective communication is fundamental in establishing a calm classroom. Clear and concise communication enhances the learning process. The Redirect Behavior Model does not always have to address disruptive behavior; it can be used for whole-class instruction (see Chapter 3), or talking with parents, administrators, and colleagues. In particular, Phase I focuses on value statement (empathy statement), appropriate behavior (action needed), and rationale (why it's important). For example, the following is an example of how Phase I can be used when addressing a parent concern:

I understand your concern regarding John's grade [empathy]. *I am so happy that we are able to have this conversation. John is very talented in his ability to process through problems* [value/empathy].

Unfortunately, John is missing some assignments, which has impacted his grade. To bring his grade up, John needs to hand in xyz assignments [action needed].

Once he hands in the xyz assignments, he will be able to recover the lost points [rationale]. *John is very capable of completing the work, and I am here to help him before and after school.*

If your school has adopted CALM Management, designate one of the Parent Teacher Organization meetings to introduce and discuss the school behavior management program. In particular, have teachers and students demonstrate how RBM will be used in the building and classrooms. Encourage parents to practice the model during the meeting and give them a copy of the Redirect Behavior Model to take home to reference when needed. Also during this time have teachers and students demonstrate the use of the PBEs. And again, have copies available for parents to take home. As a principal, encourage your teachers to reference these methods and use RBM as they are having conversations with parents, include in any mailings, and have copies and discuss progress using the model during student conferences as well.

If your school has not adopted CALM Management, I challenge you to invite parents into your classroom. Introduce them to RBM and how you address students using the model. Include how you use conversations and choices as consequences as well. This may be seen as a bold move, but it's important for the parents to understand your expectations and your philosophy. If you sense parents are interested in your methods, you may introduce RBM. You may be surprised. Parents are often relieved that you are showing you respect their children and you are doing so in a respectful manner. Highlight the main communication components—value statement, acceptable behavior, and rationale. Have copies of the model available to give to parents during student-led conferences. Provide it in your introductory letter. The idea is to let parents know your methods for behavior management and how you want to establish an inclusive classroom community.

Anytime you are able to include parents in understanding your methods and philosophy of teaching their kids, it is quite powerful—especially with the more challenging students. Do not dismiss this opportunity. Every parent cares and wants the best for their children. Their method of communicating this may look and sound different from how you approach students. But always keep in mind that parents care and want the best for their children. So, with this knowledge it may embolden you to take the extra step in including them in your classroom. If you are a little hesitant in approaching them about your methods, you can

I didn't realize how important it was to be explicit with my communication. I assumed the students knew what I expected. I then began to communicate exactly the behaviors that I expected and the students were much more successful. I can't imagine not being very specific in communicating what I need from my students regarding their behavior and academics.

Maria Reyes-Vazquez,
English, Grades 7–12

use RBM with the parents themselves. The model is founded on classic communication precepts. As parents gain more knowledge of child development, their response to their child's behavior is more supportive in allowing the students to understand the consequences of their choices.

Involving parents is a very powerful method to help students, no matter the age of the child. It is so important to begin the year with a positive phone call and introduce yourself and indicate how excited you are to have their child in your classroom. When you need to make contact regarding a concern with their behavior (written or verbal), use Phase I of RBM. Begin with a value statement: *Johnny has such great potential. He does really well at* _____ [state the behavior or talent]. *However, he has been* _____ [state the behavior], *and I need him to* _____ [state the behavior]. *This is why* _____ [state the rationale]. Again, the Redirect Behavior Model is fundamental in communicating in a clear, respectful manner.

Communication is a cornerstone for maintaining a calm classroom. Clear, concise, and explicit communication is an essential component for eliminating assumptions, alleviating barriers, and implementing inclusive practices to ensure all students feel valued and respected, and that they have an equal opportunity for a quality education.

Teacher Presence

Did you ever observe or read stories about teachers who on their first day of school walk into their classroom, and within seconds their students gravitate toward them like a magnet? They have a strong presence. Your teacher presence continuously sends intentional and/or unintentional powerful messages to your students every moment of every day. Presence takes the form of body language, emotions, and the use of your classroom space. Developing teacher presence in your classroom can be challenging at first, but the good news is that it can be developed. However, it is imperative that you establish your very own authentic presence, which will take time, patience, and not worrying about what others think of you. Focusing on your students and keeping them in the forefront of everything you do will assist in increasing your confidence and teaching practices.

After basketball practice one day, one of the girls I was coaching approached me and gave me a simple, yet profound piece of advice that I have followed to this day. While we were shooting baskets, she stopped, looked at me, and told me to be myself and teach. She continued: "We know you can play basketball, we see you do it; just teach us and be yourself." Wow! Why didn't I think of that? Yes! I can do this! I stopped worrying about what others thought of how I was teaching or coaching my students and I relied on my talents and skills. Every time I find myself doubting my abilities, I think of Cassie and her simple words of wisdom.

Teacher presence is predicated on how well the teacher has established relationships within the classroom. Presence can be a nonverbal that communicates your confidence and teacher leader presence in the classroom. For further research, I encourage you to read Amy Cuddy's *Presence: Bringing Your Boldest Self to Your Biggest Challenges.*

> Teacher presence is predicated on relationships and delivered with confidence, yet maintains an approachable and kind demeanor.

Body Language

As expected, most new teachers are nervous, anxious, and a little uncertain when starting their teaching career. This uncertainty usually shows through their body language by the crossing of the arms, hunched shoulders, head down, and lack of facial expression. Students are intuitive and will pick up on any of your uncertainties, which could negatively impact the culture of your classroom. As a new teacher you want to project a calm confidence. You can achieve this by effectively developing appropriate body language.

It starts by greeting each student at the door. When standing in front of the classroom, don't stand behind the desk. If you stand behind the desk it only places a barrier between you and the students. Stand in front and move around the classroom. Stand tall, with your shoulders back and your head held up, looking at every student. Place your hands in plain view by either keeping them to your side or bent mid-level. Try not to place your hands in your pockets or cross your arms. Placing your hands in your pockets signifies to your students that you have something to hide or you're nervous about something. Crossing your arms usually signifies to your students that you are being authoritative or defensive. This is especially true when you are dealing with a misbehaving student.

Emotions

The ability to handle conflict in the classroom is central to a CALM classroom. As mentioned throughout this book, it is imperative to handle those challenging situations in a calm manner where you are in control, yet you are providing opportunities where students are taking responsibility for their actions.

In addition to remaining calm during challenging situations, it is imperative to be a continuous observer over your own emotions throughout the teaching of content, listening to the stories of other students, and in understanding the students' backgrounds academically, behaviorally, socially, and emotionally. In addition to being consciously aware of your own emotions, you must be actively aware of your students' physical and emotional behaviors. Get to know your students by asking about how their day is going. Pay particular attention to any abrupt changes in their behavior, and immediately provide or find support, as needed.

Your emotional tone impacts the learning environment, and it can have an effect on student performance and in developing your students' social and emotional skills. According to Harvey and Evans (2003), the teacher's emotional disposition drives the classroom climate. Think about it: If you walk into your classroom grumpy about a disagreement you had with your significant other prior to school, how do you think your students will react to your grumpy mood? How do you think your grumpy mood will affect the climate in your classroom? Keeping a check on your emotions is not an easy task, but it is imperative in order to maintain a positive classroom environment.

Emotions Regarding Discipline

So often when I work with new teachers their fears are the same as for all grade-level teachers: *What if they don't do what I ask them? What if they hate me after I discipline them? I don't want them to view me as the strict, mean teacher.*

These are very real concerns for new teachers. To be liked and accepted is a natural inclination for everyone. No one goes into a situation and thinks, *I'm going in there to discipline kids and I don't care what anyone thinks of me. I'm the law and kids are going to follow my orders. If they don't they are going to get the boot.* This approach will be sure to produce adverse results in the long run.

An undisciplined classroom breeds apathy and disinterest. Students want direction. Students want a teacher to hold them accountable. Students want routines and procedures. They will test you to see how far they can take it, but deep down they want you to hold them accountable for their behavior. This was very clear when I worked with at-risk students. One may suspect that students who are facing serious challenges do not want discipline. At first they resisted. I got a lot of negative feedback from the students—grunts and groans, or a flat-out refusal to follow directions. I strongly suggest that you be persistent and work for the small wins.

> Go for the small wins, hold students accountable, and build upon each success. Eventually the small wins will become big wins.

When I was delivering the expectations to the students, I felt nervous the first time. I was just getting to know the students, and I didn't want them to think I was a "mean" teacher. But I knew I had to let them know what I expected and follow through and redirect them if they did not follow the expectations. As class progressed, I had to redirect a student. I was scared because I didn't know how he would react, but it went fairly well because I set the expectation. I always thought teachers that yelled were mean. I didn't want to be that teacher, so now I realize if I let the students know my expectations and I give a rationale, it isn't mean or strict when I have to follow through and redirect their behavior. It means I have high expectations.

Nataly Orozco,
middle level math/science

Students need to know the difference between a mistake and failure. A mistake happens; it's expected. But what's important is how a person reacts to the mistake. Are they going to take responsibility for their actions and try to do better the next time? This is where learning and growth will flourish. Or are they going to reject responsibility and blame others for their mistake? This is a tough life lesson, but it is one that, if learned early, can truly have a long-term impact on their life choices.

Also, it is important to note that once a student has been disciplined, it's over. You need to let it go. You cannot continue to "punish" a student for the infraction. However, how does the teacher handle the situation when the comment is hurtful? It sounds easy to let it go. But in reality, it can be difficult, especially if they touched upon a sensitive subject. This is when you have a couple of options. You may continue the conversation, let the student know their comments are hurtful, and try to redirect the conversation to something constructive. Or you may indicate that you and/or the student are too frustrated right now to have a respectful conversation, and to continue when you are calm.

I had a student with whom I had frequent conversations regarding her behavior. At one point, she began to make some pointed accusations about my physical appearance during class. For the most part, I can handle this, but on this particular day it was hurtful. It was evident to the student that she struck a chord with me. I ignored her comments and continued with instruction. After class we had a conversation. I took a deep breath and told her that it wasn't okay to say hurtful comments to people. I continued to remain calm and gave her time to respond. To my surprise, she looked at me and told me that she didn't mean to hurt my feelings. She went on to self-reflect on how she made assumptions about me. We discussed further how assumptions can be hurtful and shared some ideas as to how to approach this topic in the future. We made progress after that conversation, but it would have been difficult to have that conversation if we had not remained calm and established a culture based on trust and respect.

Every situation presents a unique opportunity to address behaviors. Here are a few ideas to consider:

- Take deep breaths. Slow the conversation.

- Identify that you or both of you are upset. *"Let's have the conversation when we are calm."*

- Let the student know that they hurt your feelings.

- Talk about why they are displaying the behavior.

- Talk about how they may adjust their behavior.

- Without the student present, make a plus/delta t-chart and list all the positives and the not-so-positive attributes of the student. Do this when you are calm and there has been an appropriate amount of time away from the situation.

Physical Classroom Environment

Creating a well-thought-out physical arrangement of the classroom environment plays an essential role in creating a CALM managed classroom. The structure of the classroom assists in promoting learning and can positively affect both teacher and student behavior. An organized classroom provides students predictability, accessibility, and an atmosphere where their academic, emotional, and social needs are being met—all of which enhance a CALM classroom.

> An organized classroom provides students predictability, accessibility, and an atmosphere where their academic, emotional, and social needs are being met—all of which enhance a CALM classroom.

Positive Mindset

Having a positive mindset begins internally. Positive self-talk will reduce stress levels and enable you to have a better overall attitude, which will have a positive effect on the learning environment. Negative self-talk can be detrimental to your ability to lead in a confident, calm manner. All of us have experienced negative self-talk, but the key is to stop it before it influences your attitude in the classroom. When you have a negative thought, stop yourself and focus on something positive, something general in nature. For example, if you are having trouble relating to a student who is presenting challenges, stop and focus on one or two positive features of the student. Focus on those features and the positive thoughts will gain momentum; soon you will notice more and more positive attributes from the student. A thought will gain momentum, whether it is a positive or a negative thought. Conversations carry the same momentum. If you engage in negative conversations with colleagues, the negative feelings will gain momentum and disrupt the positive energy. Focus on positive thoughts and conversations and you will notice a dramatic effect on your classroom. The positive energy will eventually replace the negative and you will have a calm, peaceful learning environment. It sounds simplistic, but I challenge you to engage in positive thoughts and conversations for a week and notice how you feel. Notice the responses from your students and colleagues. It is hard to deny that positive conversations and word choices will have a positive effect on the calm classroom. Positive thoughts and conversations will translate into a positive mindset.

Concentrate on the positive attributes of the student(s). Be careful of reviewing or listening to teachers who may have had trouble with a student the previous year. Give the student a chance before you make an assumption on their abilities, either behavior or academic. A year can make a difference in their maturation progress. Also, if you focus your energy and thoughts on a negative behavior a student may display, you will always see this behavior. It is much like the red car example in Chapter 6: If I decide I want to buy a red car, as I drive I will notice every red car on the street. When you focus your energy on something, you will begin to be more aware of its presence. If you think Johnny will never hand in an assignment on time, he will live up to your expectations.

Instruction

A CALM classroom paves the way for strong instructional strategies. The classroom may look and sound different on a daily basis. Do not mistake compliance for engagement. Students may appear compliant because they are not talking during instruction, they may appear to be taking notes, but it doesn't mean they are engaged. Are you incorporating group work, relating content to student experiences? Are students socially interacting and being given choices to share their knowledge?

A CALM classroom may look and sound different on a daily basis. Voice levels will vary according to your instruction. Some days the voice levels may be escalated because students are working in groups, but their discussions are on topic. A loud classroom may reveal that students are excited about sharing their ideas and experiences. This is great! Facilitating student conversations to ensure your instruction allows students to create a safe and supportive learning environment. When students understand your expectations and know you are going to hold them accountable you can expand the learning environment and engage them in project-based learning, inquiry-based learning, presentations, discussions, creating media, case studies, etc. Here are some items to consider when planning your lessons:

- Who is doing most of the talking?
- Transfer the talking and discussion to the students.

- Record yourself, evaluate who is doing the talking, and adjust your plans.

- Incorporate brain breaks (2–5 minutes of movement).

- Incorporate movement into your lessons (stations, projects, etc.).

- Do not talk longer than 15 minutes (differs for each age group; should not exceed the age of the youngest student).

- Let your students struggle at times; do not be quick to answer their question.

- Meet students with questions when they have a question.

- Incorporate partner and collaborative group work.

Summary

Whether you are a classroom teacher leader or a teacher leader who supports the classroom teacher with their instruction, the guiding principles apply for sound leadership in and out of the classroom. Relationships, respect, and intentional communication are elements essential to the success of the students. The Redirect Behavior Model can be instrumental in having a calm, collaborative conversation. And each decision should be based on what's best for the student.

Reflection Questions

- Think about your progression as a teacher leader. Where have you seen the most growth as a teacher leader?

- Think about a time you were a teacher leader. Was it an informal or formal role? What were your successes? What were your challenges? How might you approach the opportunity differently today?

- Take a moment to review your teaching practices. What innovative strategy have you implemented? Consider sharing it with your colleagues in your school, district, or at a conference.

Quick Wins

1. Take the time to write down your vision as a teacher. Post it and revisit periodically. It will evolve as you grow and learn from your experiences.

2. Think about a time when you were a teacher leader. Was it an informal or formal role? What were your successes? What were your challenges? How might you now approach the opportunity differently?

3. Take a risk. Set a goal that will get you out of your comfort zone and into a new environment.

Student as a Leader

Before I taught middle school I was teaching at a maximum security prison for boys ages 12–21. I tried to make my last day at the prison as routine as any other day, not informing the students of my departure. My efforts were futile, since stories at the facility flew faster than Usain Bolt sprinting for gold. After dismissing my last class, I noticed one inmate lagging behind. Devon was a tough kid, a person of few words. He had this underlying angry, emotional tilt. Every day he would complete his work, but did not add to the conversation. I really didn't think he listened, let alone cared about anything I was trying to teach. Devon made sure he was the last one out of the classroom. He stopped in front of my desk and said, "So I hear you're leaving to go teach middle school." I stuttered a shaky "Yes." I wasn't sure what to expect because I rarely heard him speak. "I wished I had had a teacher like you who held me accountable for my decisions. Someone who believed in me. Middle school was a turning point where things went bad. I wish someone like you had taken an interest, guided me. That's when I went the wrong direction." Few words, but powerful. I was absolutely speechless. Devon's words made me certain that I was in the right profession and doing the right thing for my students.

I tell that story because Devon represents a great number of the student inmates who were extremely intelligent, charismatic, and passionate. These are fantastic leadership traits. What if a teacher had intervened and created a positive environment for them to grow as people, both intellectually and ethically? What if the inmates had experienced times during their schooling when they felt like they were valued and their voices were heard and mattered? Leaders exist among our lower-achieving students, but since their talents aren't valued at school, they sometimes find other, less socially positive, ways of applying their talents. Why aren't our schools trying to tap into this resource? If we celebrated their talents and encouraged them to apply them positively to contribute to the school community, we would be fostering their growth as active, productive citizens of their community. We are missing opportunities with our students. For some, the classroom may be the only opportunity to grow and develop their leadership potential for the good of society.

Often in classrooms you will find that the high-ability learners are the students in leadership positions. These students typically are the ones who have a higher GPA, hold a leadership position on the student council, manage fund-raisers, and are active in several different school clubs and organizations. Unfortunately, there is a perception that only the talented and gifted students will make good leaders. But by overlooking the middle- and lower-level academic achievers, we are missing out on some of the most charismatic, passionate, risk-taking, and innovative leaders. By investing a little time and energy in developing leadership skills in all students, regardless of their academic status, schools have the potential of benefiting from a diverse set of student leaders. Furthermore, utilizing the leadership talents of at-risk students has the potential to get those students who are most likely to drop out reinvested in the school community.

Developing students as leaders requires developing them as citizens of high character, high-achieving learners, and valued members of their community. Student leadership involves the ability to communicate ideas and opinions, participating as an active member of the decision-making process, and understanding civic and ethical responsibilities. When students are given opportunities to lead within their school, they have a greater sense of empowerment regarding their learning environment (Black & Walsh, 2009).

A central element of leadership is learning how to lead yourself before you are able to lead others, and this begins by holding students accountable for their actions. Taking responsibility for your behavior and your learning develops confidence, a positive mindset, clear communication skills, and a positive attitude. I noticed that once students began to take ownership of their behavior and learning, their confidence levels increased and they became more outspoken about their needs and wants in the classroom.

I implemented the Student Communication Model (SCM) and the Community Council (CC) in my classrooms to ensure that all students had the opportunity to successfully hold a leadership role and learn from others. The decision to involve students more in the framework of the classroom came about because I had established a well-managed classroom. Now what? I wanted to take the next step in supporting my students in becoming more involved and accountable in the classroom. I wanted to teach them to really take control over the learning environment. Implementing SCM and CC was an integral component in assisting the transfer from a direct teaching approach to a more indirect method of teaching.

I was able to introduce more project-based learning because the students were able to work independently and in groups responsibly. The time we took in the beginning of the semester paid off within a couple of months. The classroom was calm. If they needed to be redirected I simply would remind the whole class by stating "Voices!" or "On task!" and the students knew to get back to work. By allocating some of my tasks to the students I was able to work with students who needed extra support and provide challenging extension material to those who needed it.

The Student Communication Model

When I took the time to record and analyze how my students were communicating during whole-class discussions I found that the same few voices were heard over and over again. When other students outside of this group communicated their ideas, the class would not listen or take them seriously. They were often ignored. I wanted to implement a protocol that would ensure that all voices were empowered and heard. My solution was the Student Communication Model (SCM).

The Student Communication Model is a guided script students follow to convey their ideas and opinions with great consideration for diverse perspectives. It is designed to be a simple, straightforward, 3-step process, which allows students to communicate with considerable efficiency and effectiveness. The Student Communication Model's intention is to focus the speaker's attention on one idea and to deliver the message in an efficient manner. It encourages students to voice their opinions without fear of ridicule because it requires students to acknowledge and appreciate other students' point of view, which is a critical component in respectful dialogue. Students struggle articulating their point of view. The Student Communication Model enables the student to communicate their ideas by concentrating on one thought at a time, which allows for more effective communication. It also teaches the students that it is acceptable to disagree, although the students need to learn how to voice their opinion in a respectful manner.

The Student Communication Model's main components are:

1. Offer a value statement: Recognize someone else's opinion. This diminishes the emotional struggle that may arise from differing opinions.

   I understand you may . . . [feel, think, tried, stated].

2. Propose an alternative perspective: Explicitly and unambiguously state your idea.

   But have you thought about . . . [alternative perspective]?

3. Suggest a rationale: Offer evidence that supports your new idea or opinion.

   I think this because . . . [rationale].

It did not take a great deal of time to teach, and the time was well worth the effort. It proved most effective for students who you knew had great ideas, but were not able to relay their ideas for a variety of reasons, including a lack of confidence. They let the students who were more boisterous lead the discussion and present ideas to the class. I felt this model would even the playing field. After I introduced the model, I had students talking who normally would not have had the courage.

I had a student who had difficulty expressing her ideas. She worked well in small groups, but when she offered her ideas, she was often dismissed by her peers. When she used the model, she was able to verbalize her ideas, and students began to take her more seriously. It gave her a voice. Providing this protocol for both speakers and listeners means that students' ideas don't get lost or dismissed, and it gives everyone more confidence.

The model forced students to think about the "why" of their solution. They had to take a moment to think about their ideas and articulate the rationale. Once they were able to communicate their idea supported with their rationale, it made everyone involved think about their solutions/ideas in a more thoughtful manner.

Pacing

I don't recommend introducing this model during the first few weeks of school. This model is designed to be used when you have the behaviors well managed and in control. Introduce the Student Communication Model (SCM) sometime after the students have an adequate understanding of the Positive Behavior Expectations (PBEs). Reserve a class period or introduce at the beginning of each class. Begin the process by providing students with various social issues or concepts from the curriculum for them to discuss. All grade levels and content areas may use this method. It can be a formal (debate) or informal (class conversation) setting. For example, math topics may include logic and reasoning for all grade levels. Give the students a topic that will present multiple perspectives for them to debate. Have the students practice with a partner until they are confident to demonstrate these new communication skills in a whole-group setting. At first it will sound scripted, and most students will be uncomfortable. Some students may be reluctant at first. They may exhibit negative body language such as eye rolls and shifting in seats. All of this is to be expected. Do not let it deter you from going forward. Embrace the challenge. Support the students through positive reinforcement, be patient, and believe that you and your students will be able to persevere and achieve stronger communication skills over time.

Quick Wins

Novice teachers may not introduce this model until the second semester or second year. Concentrate on establishing and maintaining behavior expectations and progressing with instructional strategies.

> Teaching this model can take 20 minutes. Make sure to follow through and have the students use the model. Students catch on quite quickly.

When you're ready to implement, try putting a poster of the Student Communication Model on the wall for students to reference. Eventually the students will be able to practice SCM in a calm, confident manner. An increase in confidence will result in a more conversational tone. As student confidence increases, consider opening each class with a scenario for students to practice SCM in pairs. As they become more proficient in their delivery, begin implementing the model in whole-group settings.

The Student Communication Model may be used anytime students are engaged in conversation. Students will become so adept at using the model that it will appear seamless in delivery. It works well with 1:1 conversations, collaborative work groups, whole-group discussions, discussion with respect to highly sensitive topics, and is an outstanding option for debates.

The Student Communication Model also works well as a model for students to come up with solutions to their own problems. Establish the expectation that when a student comes to you with a problem, they will first develop a proposed solution to the problem. The student should ask, "What am I going to do about it?" This is an exercise in applying critical thinking, self-reliance, agency, and independence. Having the expectation that students will apply SCM to their problems communicates that you trust students to take on the responsibility of resolving their own problems. For example, a student is having difficulty accepting the written feedback they received from the teacher. The student may approach the teacher, and it may sound like this: *I understand and accept most of the feedback you provided* [empathy], *but I am struggling with this feedback* [shows the feedback] *in particular. I was thinking that the author was inferring a peaceful resolution* [alternative perspective]. *I thought when the author noted how the sun came up and the birds were chirping, that implied there was peace and the conflict was resolved* [rationale].

High school students may at first display a reluctance to use SCM. Follow through with the students to follow the model. It is easy to dismiss it, but remember that this is a skill they can use throughout their entire life. Encourage them and guide them through the first iterations. Eventually the students will prompt one another to use the model.

I used the Student Communication Model for our Socratic Seminar. The students were more deliberate in proposing their thoughts and ideas. We were able to dive deeper into the content because the model guided their conversation.

Andrew Ciochetto, middle level science

Students may be reluctant at first. Remember, the ability to articulate your ideas is a skill that will benefit them beyond the classroom.

Ideas for Elementary Students

- Have the sentence starters posted for students to reference
  - *I understand . . .*
  - *But have you thought about . . .*
  - *I think this because . . .*

Ideas for Middle School/High School Students

- Use the model for debate scenarios

- Use the model for writing exercises

  - Quick write

  - Proof statement

Community Council

The legendary coach of the Nebraska Cornhuskers, Dr. Tom Osborne, wanted to put a system in place so that student athletes could hold one another accountable for their actions on and off the field—as teammates, academic students, and citizens of the community. He created the Unity Council to empower his athletes to monitor each other's behavior and academic achievements through a point system. The main idea Coach Osborne wanted to convey was that each player had a voice; they were heard and valued. After he created the Unity Council in 1991, he went on to win three National Championships during the 1990s.

I loved this idea. The Unity Council represented much of what I was trying to convey to my students. I wanted them to increase their involvement, feel valued, make their voices heard, and I wanted to create a team atmosphere where classmates were willing to hold one another accountable for their academics and behavior. However, I did not want this to pit students against one another; nor did I want to begin policing and punishing students. Instead, I offered a platform for students to hold one another accountable, but instituted a protocol for them to follow in which I would be the ultimate decision maker. Instead of telling my students what I wanted to accomplish, I put theory into practice and had the students create a Community Council. The whole class agreed upon the weekly academic and behavior goals, and when they achieved their goals they were eligible to participate in the Kickback Friday activities. The Community Council decided what the team building activity would be for the Kickback Friday event.

Purpose of the Community Council

The goal of the Community Council (CC) is to develop students as leaders by having the students accept responsibility for their academic progress and their behavior. The Community Council empowers students to cocreate a culture of support and motivate their peers to improve their behavior and academics. The council leader's goal is to lead their group in discussion on a variety of topics, which may include: potential changes or suggestions for an assignment, making an adjustment or sharing new ideas for an extension activity (see Chapter 9), service to others, kindness projects, or behavior.

Appointing the Council Leader

Divide the class into groups of four to six students. Each group elects a council leader. The council leader will rotate every month or two to ensure that all students in each group have an opportunity to serve as a council leader.

When the Council Convenes

At the beginning of the week, the CC will meet for 10 minutes as a whole class and the teacher will guide the CC to develop weekly academic and behavioral goals. These goals will be different for each class, depending on the needs of the students. Throughout each week, the council leaders will meet with their respective groups to discuss their progress and will make any adjustments necessary within their group to ensure their peers are successfully meeting the classroom goals. The council leaders report to each other and to the teacher their group's progress. Overall, the students are at the center of the decision making and conversations; however, the teacher is the ultimate decision maker.

The council leader has various duties, including:

- Lead council meetings
- Gather group ideas

- State solution(s) to the class

- Implement the Student Communication Model (SCM) and/or the Positive Behavior Expectations (PBEs)

Community Council Whole-Class Meeting Protocol

Developing a routine CC protocol will allow for consistency and efficiency. This protocol is developed as a whole class to ensure inclusion and increase the understanding of the CC. Here is an example:

- A CC meeting is requested (by student or teacher).

- The council leader announces the reason for the meeting of the whole class. Often, students have already talked about the reason for a meeting.

- Council leaders will meet with their small groups to gather their ideas/solutions.

- Council leaders use SCM to share their ideas/solutions with the whole class.

- Teacher uses questioning prompts to fill in any gaps that the students may not have considered.

- Teacher asks the council leaders for their final ideas/solutions.

- Teacher has the final decision of the ideas/solutions.

Addressing Whole-Class Behavior: In addition to academics, the council addresses behavior as a whole class. For example, you could start off by working on one PBE, set a goal, and have the council organize the class incentive for attaining that goal. A goal for the class might be to have on-topic conversations during collaborative work groups. The teacher's role is to observe and monitor the groups, allowing the council leaders to address any issues regarding on-topic conversations. As the teacher, there may be times you have to prompt the council leaders to address their groups to have on-topic conversations.

Peer and Self-Regulate: Have students self- and peer regulate by having students prompt one another if they are not following the expectation. It is the same process as teaching students to give peer feedback. Give the students a chance to self-correct.

Leadership Skills Developed: One important aspect of improving student leadership skills is for them to develop calm, clear, concise communication. A good resource for students to use is SCM, which will help them articulate their ideas in a more mature and calm manner. The Student Communication Model will also assist them to think through their thoughts and have a rationale to back up their message. In fact, using SCM will explicitly call for students to reiterate what the other person just communicated, which is the direct result of having developed good listening skills. Students can also use the Positive Behavior Expectations (PBEs) in establishing a culture of respect—in particular, the skill of listening. The council protocol is to allow all leaders to communicate their ideas without interruption and apply the skill of listening. By utilizing both SCM and PBEs, students will be able to communicate effectively in a safe, supportive environment.

Adjustments: In order to maintain success with the CC, have the students concentrate on one behavior and one academic expectation for each week. Keep it simple and measurable. As much as you work to develop students as leaders, there are some students who may require additional attention, especially in regard to their behavior. The idea of the council is to have students accept responsibility for their learning environment regarding their behavior and academic achievements. For the council to be successful, it is imperative that the Positive Behavior Expectations have been well established and the majority of the students are following them without prompt.

The Community Council will vary greatly with grade levels. For example, for elementary students, you may identify a leader for the day, and their potential duties could consist of door holder, pencil patrol, calendar helper, line leader, and teacher helper. Obviously, as the students get older their responsibilities as council leader will grow.

Teacher Role

In order for you to be able to successfully implement the CC, you have to have established yourself as a strong teacher leader and have a well-managed classroom. The council is not developed to relieve your duties as a teacher. As mentioned, the goal of the CC is to develop students as leaders by having the students accept responsibility for their academic progress and their behavior. If you find the CC is taking too much class time, you may want to rethink the council. The council is not in place to take away class time, but to serve as a platform to empower students, develop them as leaders, and motivate them to do better with their behavior and academics.

Incentive

As previously mentioned, the whole class will create their weekly academic and behavioral goals. If the whole class achieves their goals for the week, you want to ensure there is an incentive for them achieving their goals. For example, I used Kickback Friday events (see Chapter 9 for Kickback Friday details). Keep it simple. Weekly goals and rewards work well together.

My class consists of a diverse group of learners with varying levels of academic and social needs. I implemented the Community Council to teach my students how to take ownership of their behavior and academic needs. I knew that if I had them more involved in the CALM Classroom process their behavior would improve, which would impact their academic success. Dr. Lentfer actually implemented the council in our undergraduate class. It worked well with our class, and I liked how it made us responsible and accountable for our actions. Yet, ultimately we knew Dr. Lentfer, as the teacher, would have the last word on what would actually be enacted. We tried to present the need for a food day once a week. We presented our ideas, but Dr. Lentfer rejected the idea. But she rejected it through a series of questions that led us to realizing how food would result in our learning progression.

I took this council concept into my classroom. I felt that my students were in need of a system to self-regulate and be able to hold one another accountable to further the idea of working collaboratively with one another. I implemented the council with each of my classes, but each class presented different needs and issues. I made adjustments for each class. For the lower-achieving class in respect to their behavior and academics, I designated a time each week to review our class goals. I did not have the students meet without my interacting with them. They maintained their small groups with a leader, but we did more of a whole-class interaction. I would adjust my involvement according to their behavior abilities.

I noticed a sense of ownership and an increase in student engagement. Prior to the council I felt like I was leading the initiatives that would motivate the students. Their behavior would fall into place, and the transition from helpless learner to an independent learner was extraordinary.

Andrew Ciochetto,
middle level science

Summary

Creating a Community Council (CC) not only provides the opportunity for all students to develop successful leadership skills, but empowers them to cocreate a culture of support and motivate their peers to improve their behavior and academics. By implementing the council, students will have the opportunity to play an active role in applying SCM and PBEs, and they will begin to self-regulate their behavior in a more positive manner.

Reflection Questions

- Think about a time you had a challenging student who was humorous and whom students liked to follow. How could you use them to channel their talents? Could a leadership role assist in using their talents?

- What holds you back from giving students more decision-making power? Are your fears based on perceptions from colleagues? Administrators? District testing time? Students' abilities?

- What would be the worst-case scenario if you implemented SCM and/or CC?

- What would be the best outcome from implementing SCM and/or CC?

- How can we balance our instruction to involve developing students as citizens, as leaders, and as academic achievers?

Quick Wins

- Start slow with the CC. Implement portions of the council one at a time and build upon each component.

- Teach a few students SCM, then have those students teach two other students. Continue until all have encountered the model.

PART IV

MOTIVATION

Motivation Plan

>> Motivation—the elusive mystery as to how to engage the disengaged
and inspire the uninspired.

I observe behavior around me all the time. I have implemented motivational programs (discussed in this chapter), but I believe the best way to motivate students is to be the most authentic, caring version of you. It's in the simple things—a smile, a compliment, a please, a thank you. It's in teaching with love and kindness in your heart, not "gotcha"-motivated assessments or veiled threats of do this or something extremely terrible is going to happen—which do nothing to motivate a student except the direct opposite.

I always described myself as a good/bad student. I was a good student in that I didn't have a bad attitude. I didn't hate school; I just didn't always like how teachers treated me. I admit that I was ornery; I tested the limits of many of my teachers. But the teachers who motivated me were the ones who understood me, believed in me, encouraged me, and valued me. My biology and English teachers had different styles, but they had the same message—I care about you. My biology teacher embraced my humor, and he compromised with me. I had to stay quiet and take notes during instruction, and at the end of the class he gave me time to do my imitation of him teaching. It may sound horrible, but my imitation was not mean spirited; I actually reviewed the lesson, and everyone had a good laugh (he tricked me!). Oh, and he moved me from the back to the front of the class (classic teacher move, but one that worked). My

English teacher inspired me. She loved her content, she loved her students, and she had a wonderful sense of humor. She could teach like no other teacher. She held us to high standards, and I wanted desperately to meet her expectations. I wanted to because I admired the way she held herself and conveyed the message—I believe in you. Not many teachers did that when I was in high school. To be fair, I didn't give them a chance to believe in me (that story in my next book!).

I have found that with all of my students—from those who were incarcerated to those who were extremely gifted and talented—just like me, all of them needed one thing—someone who believed in them without judgment. Show them that you care with humor, understanding, and compassion. Just because you smile or are able to laugh with your students doesn't mean that you are soft or a pushover. It means you are relating to them. You are human. You can still hold them to high expectations, but do it without yelling and demeaning words. I know it can be frustrating at times. Step away and put things into perspective. They are kids. They are learning and developing physically and socially. They are going to make mistakes. They should make mistakes. And guess what? So are you. No need to take their mistakes personally. No need to get angry because Johnny never turned in the correct assignment even after you told him to turn it in six times. Tell him seven times and teach him why it's important to turn in the correct assignment. If you can't explain the why, then maybe you shouldn't have assigned the work in the first place.

You may say, "This all sounds great, but you don't know what it's like." And I can tell you, "Yes, I do." I have made the rookie mistake of giving treats as an incentive/reward, went broke, had kids go on a sugar high, and faced a chaotic classroom. I became a better teacher when I quit worrying about the standards. I believed in the curriculum the district created because I knew the curriculum would address and meet the state standards. So I let it go. I relaxed and focused my energy on something that was missing: fun. Isn't that the ultimate motivator? I looked at my seventh graders and knew they needed to move around and play. I incorporated play, also known as team-building strategies, which I offer as some of my strategies in this chapter. We did everything from impromptu strategies to yoga in my class. And the students still met and exceeded their state test goals. Motivation doesn't need to be fancy and expensive. Motivation is right at your fingertips. It's knowing your students and building a classroom culture that is safe to celebrate the mistakes and successes, encourage students to explore and embrace life as an adventure, and always to find the fun.

Intrinsic motivation comes from within the student; they are driven by internal rewards rather than external rewards (extrinsic motivation). By going through the steps of RBM and holding themselves accountable for their actions, students get into the habit of making better choices. By making better choices, the student's behavior, relationships, self-esteem, and the overall community of the classroom improve, which in turn is internally rewarding to the student. For example, when a student chooses to participate in a group project they develop a sense of pride in contributing and a sense of belonging in the classroom community. That sense of pride and belonging internally motivates the student to adopt future positive behaviors. The Redirect Behavior Model emphasizes giving students a choice to act in prosocial ways or antisocial ways. Once students accept that they have the agency to act and realize they will face consequences based on their choices, chances are they will be empowered to make choices that benefit them.

I grew up on a farm near Strang, Nebraska. The town had one school—four rooms with two full-time teachers, a K–third-grade teacher and a fourth-grade–eighth-grade teacher. I brought the lessons I learned in my small-town community to my big-city classroom.

Strang was a farming community where everyone pitched in for sporting events, PTA meetings, plays, holiday celebrations, and during adverse circumstances. At the end of the school year, the students (all 17 of us), parents, teachers, and all community members would work to clean the town. We would pick up trash along the single mile surrounding the town and all of the roads within the town. We trimmed trees, painted buildings, and cleaned restrooms. And at the end of the day we would light a huge bonfire and roast hotdogs to celebrate the day's work. I loved that day. It was fun to work with parents and community members (people who didn't even have kids but cared about the community) to clean the town. That sounds crazy, that adolescents enjoyed manual labor and picking up trash, but it gave us an overwhelming sense of pride in our community. This sense of pride is what motivated us all to pitch in. This was the very feeling I wanted to instill in my students.

We emphasized the *we* and not the *me*. We were held accountable for our actions, and our responsibility was to our team. We were held accountable for our position responsibilities, we pushed one another to be better athletes and people, and we dropped our egos to work as one for the ultimate goal of winning. But in a classroom, what were we going to win, and against whom were we going to compete? State tests could be the equivalent of the state tournament. Unit tests were similar to conference games. Now I just had to figure out how to motivate them to do well on the tests as a team.

Motivation is seen as the impetus to a learning environment that embraces a constructivist view integrating different theories relating to cognitive, achievement, and social factors (Bryan, Glynn, & Kittleson, 2011; Jones, 2014). The self-determination theory focuses primarily on student intrinsic and extrinsic motivation (Deci, Vallerand, Pelletier, & Ryan, 1991; Jones, 2008). This theory contends simply that intrinsically motivated students are driven by internal rewards and extrinsically motivated students will engage in an activity because they want to complete it for an outcome from outside of themselves (Deci & Ryan, 2000). Students are intrinsically motivated when they are able to engage in choice, when they are able to regulate their actions in a more self-determined manner because they were able to have a choice in their learning activity (Deci et al., 1991; Deci & Ryan, 1985).

Both intrinsic and extrinsic motivation are beneficial for students. It is important for the teacher to create a balance between the two types of motivation, and to know when to use external or internal motivation. At first, a teacher may entice students with a reward system. This is fine, but know that this is a temporary fix for a long-term phenomenon. Your main goal is to intrinsically motivate students. Rewarding students for their efforts with food, for example, will extrinsically motivate them, but the feeling of accomplishment will be associated with a treat, not learning. Plus, if you solely rely on something like food for a reward, you will notice your checking account take a big hit. Rewarding students with food is fine on occasion, but we need to think beyond the moment and get the students to become intrinsically motivated in order to achieve and improve their behavior and academics.

Motivation Plan—Whole Class

Setting Behavioral Goals

Motivating students means purposely creating a learning environment where students are engaged in setting their own goals (both for behavioral improvement and academic achievement) and are held accountable for their behavior. Setting their own goals has been shown intrinsically to have a positive impact on student motivation while promoting self-awareness (Zimmerman, 2008).

Developing behavior goals may refer to a specific PBE. For example, the class agreed to work on the specific PBE, on-topic conversations. We agreed to focus on the conversations during small-group work. Often, the students would self-regulate one another because they were motivated to earn the incentive, they knew the expectations for achieving the goal, and the time was appropriate (within a week). The students initiated the decision on what behavior they needed to work on and set the goal. I did not interfere, got out of their way, and gave them autonomy. The more I gave them space, the more they responded with higher expectations. I let it grow organically, so each class was different. I handed this over to the students because this was their classroom. I wanted them to be the creators of their space.

Check for Understanding

Verify that students have internalized the PBEs. Have students engage in role-play, discuss their goals with a partner or small group, write or draw pictures on a poster to display the behavior expectations, or they may record themselves describing the goals. All of these elements will help students to internalize their goals. Never assume students understand. Always model, discuss, and have students demonstrate comprehension.

Choices

As I mentioned earlier, by using RBM, where you give the student choices and make them accountable for their actions, students begin to learn from their mistakes, and therefore make better choices. When the student makes a positive choice and you positively reinforce their choice and behavior, this assists in intrinsically motivating them to continue on that path of making better choices. The important idea is the student makes their choice and they are in complete control of their behavior, which assists in intrinsically motivating the student. Better choices lead a student down the path to establishing better relationships among their peers—an increase in their self-esteem—and they become a valuable team member in the classroom community. If students are having difficulty coming to a consensus regarding their choice, you can even call a CC meeting and delegate the situation to the leaders. Of course, this is done with caution. You never want to publicly bring negative attention to a student, for this will have the opposite effect to intrinsically motivating a student.

Mascot

Choose a mascot for your classroom. Have some fun. I had a 5-foot skeleton made out of plywood of a tyrannosaurus rex. We named him T-Dog. The students would dress him up for each holiday. I would refer to him during instruction, and the students got a kick out of it. Keep things simple. Not everything has to have a grand scheme. You can have some fun.

Motto

Have a class motto for the year. Have a tagline that describes what you are striving for, like Nike's *Just Do It* slogan. Here are some other slogans: *One Team, One Dream*; *Teamwork Makes the Dreams Work*; *We Are One Team*. The list can go on, but have a motto that represents what you want to achieve in the classroom. The Nebraska volleyball team's motto for 2017 was *With Each Other, for Each Other*. That motto was evident during some of their toughest matches. It focused their efforts and reminded them that it was a total team endeavor. Their hard work won them the National Championship. Again, have fun with it and weave that theme into your coursework.

Inspirational Stories

Consider opening class with a short, inspirational story. Have students read them, or you can read the story. And have them do a quick write or a class discussion. The idea is to present stories that show how people under challenging situations persevered. Relate it to your classwork and how they too can persevere through hard work. I found these stories engaged the students and provided another way to support the disengaged learner.

Quick Wins

Novice Teacher: Begin the process by analyzing your lesson plans. Are your plans engaging? Are you doing most of the talking? Try to work toward a 10:2 or 15:2 teaching pacing. Ten minutes of teaching and 2 minutes of movement; incorporate brain breaks; eventually progress to team-building activities. Team-building activities can only be implemented if you are able to manage the behavior.

Reward—Kickback Friday

Work hard, play hard. Have an incentive system in place. When my students were able to achieve their goal(s) for the week we would have "Kickback Fridays." If it was nice outside, the list of activities consisted of playing soccer, kickball, tug-of-war, or any team-oriented game that incorporated all of the students. Sometimes we would stay inside playing board games, puzzles, or cribbage, chess, and checker tournaments.

Students would begin to plan for Friday events on Monday by engaging in the CC protocol. The only rule was that everyone had to participate. Every once in a while, students would fall behind on their academic/behavioral goals, but it only took a simple reminder about Kickback Fridays and they would get back on track.

One of the many things I loved about Kickback Fridays was that the students learned valuable lifelong skills. For example, there were times I would let them argue about what the Friday activity would be, which taught

Tell me, I'll forget

Show me, I'll remember

Involve me, I'll understand

Chinese proverb

the valuable lesson of compromise. Students also learned how to problem-solve, negotiate, and interpret and follow the rules. I would also allow students to referee the activities. It may be difficult for teachers to refrain from stepping in too soon, but I trained myself only to interfere when the situation escalated to the point where it looked like a fight might ensue. There is value in having students self-regulate with their academics and their play.

Everything I did in the classroom was intentional. The outdoor and indoor activities had a purpose, which was to develop skills such as how to be competitive, strategic, supportive, and problem-solvers. Teaching those skills not only plays a valuable part for our students to be successful, it also plays a part to internally motivate them to be better students and citizens in our society.

Ideas for Elementary School

- Maintain a chart for their behavior and academic goals.

- Consider adjusting the Kickback Friday to a daily reward—reserve 15 minutes at some point during the day to reward behavior and/or academic goals.

- Consider adjusting the Kickback Friday to a reward for Wednesday and Friday.

- Concentrate on one behavior and one academic goal for the class.

Ideas for Middle School

- Consider adjusting the timeline for every 2 weeks.

- Consider adjusting the time of play to 40 minutes every other Friday.

- Consider adjusting the time of play to 20 minutes once a week.

- Have students keep track of their progress.

Ideas for High School

- Try to stay away from giving them free time for 20 minutes—get them involved and participating in the team-building activity.

- Consider adjusting the timeline for every 2 weeks.

- Consider adjusting the time of play to 40 minutes every other Friday.

- Consider adjusting the time of play to 20 minutes once a week.

- Have students keep track of their progress.

Free time as a reward can be more chaotic and stressful for the teacher. It sounds like it would work, but it doesn't. Have some options for the students to do—board games, whole-class activity. Maintain this one rule—everyone has to participate.

Disengaged Student—Work for Wins

There are a multitude of reasons why students become disengaged in their learning. There are several approaches you may use to handle this situation, but whatever method you choose, know that it's going to take time to get them to engage. It may take several approaches, but it is important to note that under no circumstances will you give up on that student.

Take the time to talk to the student. The Redirect Behavior Model will allow you to indicate to the student exactly what they need to do to be successful. Using conversations as the consequence will allow you and the student to get to the heart of the situation. Build upon the student's successes.

You have to work for wins. Start with small wins and build to the wins that will eventually lead to developing skills and motivation for the student to become a self-starter. If a student comes to class without any materials and sleeps throughout the class, have the student bring a pencil. They don't have to use it; just have them bring a pencil. The student brings the pencil, and that's a win. Progress from there and ask them to bring a pencil and a piece of paper. Again, the student doesn't have to use them; just bring those two items. The student brings those two items. Again, it's a win! Build upon that and ask the student to bring those two items, and now you ask them to use the two items and take notes. You may have to tell the student to use the items for 10 minutes total during a class. You may suggest the student use the 10 minutes during instruction where they can take notes. The student performs your request. Again, it's a win.

This is an example at one end of the spectrum. The point of the example is that you need to work for wins. Students need to feel like they can achieve. That certainly does not mean you are going to continue to lower the bar. You are working to get the student at a level where they are able to develop an achievable level of motivation. You are meeting the student at their motivational level. Start small and build.

> Work for wins pertains to Pre-K–12 students. Start where they are now according to their behavior and build upon each success. It takes time. Be patient and diligent in holding the student accountable.

It is so easy to fall prey to the sheer panic of the testing schedule. I agree; this is a real concern. But there is a certain balance between teaching and shoving content down students' throats at all costs. I know at the secondary level you don't have much time, but try to incorporate some engaging team-building activities. The activities don't have to take a great deal of time, they don't have to be implemented every week, but try to do an activity once a month. And then attach one behavior or academic goal with the activity. The incentive has to be timely—if you wait too long between the goal and its end date, students will lose interest and forget about the reward. Keep it timely and relevant.

Disengaged Student—Mentor Tutoring

The disengaged student, in particular, presents a unique challenge. Motivating a disengaged student is an incremental, shaping process, which more often than not needs to begin using extrinsic motivational techniques.

My Kickback Fridays made a considerable difference in motivating my students. However, every year I would have a student who presented an extra challenge. Often their home life was less than ideal, and I noticed they were not committed to the behavior and academic expectations of the classroom. I knew I had to approach their needs with extraordinary care: I had to design a unique plan that addressed their specific challenges.

I began to brainstorm. They struggled with feelings of inadequacy, doubt, fear of failure and/or success. I wanted something in place to lift them up, help them to feel valued, to have a purpose. I began to think about what makes people feel better about themselves: responsibility. I was going to give them responsibility with a purpose. I didn't want to have some meaningless task like handing out materials or collecting finished work from the class. It had to have a purpose—a real purpose. When you give your time to help others, you give yourself purpose. To think beyond yourself can give you a profound sense of pride and can have a profound, positive effect on your self-perception and attitude. In addition, when you begin to help others you tend to forget how horrible your life is, and even, in some cases, realize your life isn't that bad, after all.

One successful way I found to motivate the disengaged student was by inspiring that student to help others, to think beyond themselves, which in turn eventually internally motivated them to improve their academic and behavior skills in and out of the classroom. So, I began placing these students in tutoring positions to help other students.

By placing students in a tutoring position, their academic skills, behavioral skills, self-esteem, and level of motivation can have a positive impact on student success. As I mentioned earlier, the disengaged student lacks confidence and struggles with senses of inadequacy, doubt, and fear. The one thing you never want to do with a disengaged student is place them in a situation where they continue to hide behind their fears and struggles. The reason why these students are disengaged is largely due to their lack of self-confidence and a bucketload of fear. I realize these students can be challenging, but with a little persistence and stretching them beyond their comfort level, these students will eventually come around.

Tutoring sessions can occur within or outside of the classroom. If you choose outside of the classroom, it may take a little planning and the ability to work with another teacher and staff member. Ideally, you will want to work with a teacher who is likeminded, someone willing to take a risk and innovative in thought and action. For example, a seventh-grade math teacher might collaborate with a fifth-grade language arts teacher. Most often, the tutoring topic should be determined by the needs of the younger student. However, if the mentor has a decent grasp of a concept, but needs a little extra practice, that concept could be the topic on which they work. For example, if the mentor needs extra practice adding fractions and the mentee struggles with adding fractions, that concept would benefit both students.

It is critical you have a solid framework in place so that the tutoring sessions can move as smoothly as possible.

Note: You are working with students who probably have had very few opportunities to be a tutor. In fact, these students may not perform to your expectations, at times, especially in the beginning. Be patient. Utilize RBM, Phase II. Ask them what happened, what might be a better choice, and why. This is a learning moment. Take this opportunity and guide the student to Do the Right Thing, Make Good Choices. You may even have the student practice SCM with their mentee. This offers a wonderful chance for them to develop their communication skills with the goal of becoming a leader on the CC. The Community Council could be one of those extrinsic motivational long-term goals for the student. Remember, at the beginning your extrinsic motivators are going to be your primary motivators to get the students to participate. Over time, you will want to wean them off the extrinsic motivators.

Framework. It is important to have a strong framework to begin building your plan. The Mentor Tutoring plan (see Figure 9.1) provides a structure and ensures efficiency for everyone involved. It will be helpful in communicating the expectations for the personnel and students.

> No matter how large or small the project is, focus attention on giving the student responsibility.

FIGURE 9.1   Mentor Tutoring Plan

Who	Action	Behavior Expectation	Action	Academic Expectation	When
William	will increase	on-task behavior	and complete	the daily assignments	by the end of one class period a week
Aisha	will utilize the	steps to getting the teacher's attention	and complete	five problems a day	by the end of one class period a week
Purpose: The purpose is to _____ [insert action] and _____ [insert behavior/academic expectation].					
Outcome: Develop _____'s [insert student name] ability to _____ [state behavior expectation] and _____ [state academic expectation] by _____ [state target date].					

Figure 9.1 provides an example of a framework that you could create to guide your students' tutoring sessions. Keep it simple. Don't get caught up in making sure the wording is perfect. If you spend too much time worrying about the wording, projects will sit idle as only a thought. Think action. Get this project going. Even after you have organized and created a sound framework, some things won't go as planned. Identify the problem and adjust the plan accordingly.

Key objectives to consider in forming your own tutoring plan:

- Purpose

  Clearly state what your purpose is for developing the plan. The disengaged student is the antithesis for the project, but what is the purpose for that particular student? Keep it simple. It could be as simple as:

  The purpose of the Mentor Tutoring plan is to increase on-task behavior.

  Or

  The purpose of the Mentor Tutoring plan is to have the student complete their daily assignments.

- Outcome

  The outcome statement needs to be descriptive, specific, and measureable. Remember, your target audience is the reluctant learners, so you will want to start slow and build upon their successes. Each plan should include a behavior and academic outcome.

The outcome for the Mentor Tutoring plan is to develop ___'s [insert student name] ___ ability to ___ [state behavior expectation]___ and ___ [state academic expectation]___ by ___ [state target date]___.

- Time

  Developing the schedule and communicating the schedule are key for success. Here are some ideas to consider while thinking about your time. When everyone has agreed upon the schedule, stick to it. Do not falter from the schedule. If you do so, communicate immediately. When you communicate, state the time change, reason for change, and a potential solution.

  o When will the students tutor? Offer specific day/week and time of day.

  o When will the teachers be notified if the student is coming to tutor? (The tutoring session is dependent on their performance in the classroom.)

  o Time to practice the tutoring session with the students and staff. Practice:

    - Walking to the tutoring location
    - Beginning the tutoring session
    - Closing the tutoring session (5-minute enjoyable activity)
    - Interpreting the outcome for each tutoring session
    - On-task behavior
    - Staff signature for tutoring session
    - Thanking the staff monitoring the tutoring session
    - Walking back to their rooms
    - Where to hand in the tutoring form

- Goals

  The student and teacher together will designate the time to establish the goals for each week. The goals will focus on behavior and academic skills. The student may be struggling with several issues but work on one behavior. Make it clear which steps the student will need to accomplish in order to attain the goal. Have the student keep track of the goal.

Teach the student to initiate the conversation regarding their goals. Implement RBM, Phase II, to prompt students with questions regarding their progress.

- Students

  The tutor is the disengaged student. They may not be involved in many activities after school, and they lack intrinsic motivation regarding behavior and academic achievement. The mentee is the student who may need a little extra help in a specific subject. The mentee is not in the same classroom as the tutor.

- Staff

  This staff is the third party who will be monitoring the tutoring session. The mentor and mentee will be well trained as to how to conduct a tutoring session prior to the session. This will allow the staff to monitor their tutoring session indirectly. The staff will not be expected to sit with the students during the tutoring session. They will be able to continue their work and watch and listen from afar. But this will only be successful if the teachers have taken the time to practice and communicate the expectations clearly with the students.

- Tutoring location

  This is contingent on the staff member or faculty member who will be monitoring the tutoring session. It could be at the library, counselor's office, with a teacher who has a plan, principal's staff, etc.

- Choice

  Offer the students choices in the content materials or the puzzle they work on at the end of the session. Choices offer autonomy and challenge students to confidently coconstruct knowledge utilizing a method with which they are most comfortable.

- Incentive system or tracking system

  This correlates with the goals. The goals will need to be measureable. This could be raising their hand to talk in class. If the student did zero blurt-outs, they achieved their goal. The student could track their progress through the use of tally marks on a goal sheet.

> Invite the student to brainstorm ideas for their project.

Getting disengaged students involved in tutoring is just one component in getting them internally motivated academically and behaviorally. Throughout this process or any other similar process you decide to use, you always want to continue to use the Redirect Behavior Model (RBM) along with the PBE model. In reaching the disengaged student, I have had 100% success using the tutoring sessions in conjunction with RBM and the PBEs. Remember, your ultimate goal should be to eliminate those extrinsic motivators and get the students to where they are actively engaged in the learning process because it is personally rewarding to them.

Ideas for Elementary School

- Instead of mentoring a student, consider having them work with a staff member.

- They could help organize books and office/class materials, perform office aid, etc.

- Match the interests of the student with the appropriate staff member:
  - Librarian
  - Administrative staff
  - Art teacher
  - Physical education teacher
  - Music teacher

Ideas for Middle School

- Have the student work with a teacher on the same team.

- Develop an art project that would encompass the entire school, such as a mural.

Ideas for High School

- Try working with another teacher.

- If there is not a teacher, reserve some time (15 minutes on a Friday) for the student to work on a project within your own class.

- If possible, try to create a project that would help other students or the community. For example, direct a food drive, clothing drive, or pen pal for soldiers in the military.

Summary

Relationships, conversations, and time will lead you to ideas on how to motivate students. Conversations lead to a better understanding of the student, their circumstances, and what their interests are. Use that information to frame your lessons and activities. Celebrate the wins and encourage students to take risks. All of us had to learn how to get beyond obstacles. Teach them to go around, over, or through those obstacles. Share stories of where you struggled. Tell them strategies you used to get through a challenging situation. Offer how you felt once you overcame the situation.

Whether you use all or parts of the strategies presented, the message is to try new strategies to motivate students. Have fun. Get the students involved in helping you devise a plan.

It's a process. It doesn't happen overnight. Meet the student where they are now in behavior and academics. And work for wins. Start small and progress for the big wins.

Reflection Questions

- How might students respond if you involved them in deciding on an incentive activity?

(Continued)

(Continued)

- Have you ever tried to employ any motivation program within your class? Your school?

- What do you think the worst outcome would be if you implemented a motivation reward system? What do you think the best outcome would be? Are you willing to try implementing a motivation reward system?

- What resources do you have that could help you to develop a motivation program?

Quick Wins

1. Begin class by reading an inspirational story—one that has characters and/ or dilemma with which your students can identify. Have students write about or discuss the story. This does not have to take more than 5 minutes. Sharing stories where people overcome difficult challenges can offer students inspiration to achieve.

2. Have students share an experience where they overcame an obstacle. Have the students write their story and encourage them to share with a partner, small group, or whole class. Model an experience you had overcoming an obstacle. Consider sharing what appears to be a small or insignificant obstacle and how you learned from that experience. Focus on teaching the how and why you overcame an obstacle. This will especially help the disengaged student who may have difficulty understanding the key elements needed to persevere. Students will be able to relate to you and your story, which will further the idea of building relationships and modeling how you overcame your circumstances.

3. Consider adding the following games to your classroom:

   a. Cribbage boards, chess, checkers, cards, Jenga, board games, jigsaw puzzles, dominoes, Boggle

   b. Utilize competition—cribbage tournaments, chess tournaments, etc.

10 Final Thoughts

Key Takeaways

I shared a great deal of my first-year experiences. I did this to show the progression of how I arrived at creating my CALM Management tools. Often you learn the most from your most challenging moments, and this is where a great deal of my communication tools were developed. Because of these challenging situations I was able to develop these tools and experience great success as well.

I felt compelled to write this book because I believe very strongly in preparing new teachers and veteran teachers to be the best they can be for themselves and the students. I teach undergraduate students preparing to become K–12 teachers. I have had the privilege to have these students participate in an extensive field practicum in which they are teaching and coteaching with their mentor teacher every day for 6 weeks. This allowed the students to put CALM Management theory into practice. Their growth and confidence grew through this experience, and I was also able to adjust my strategies to meet the changing needs of the students.

You can use these tools in the beginning of the year, in the middle, or even toward the end of the year or semester. The strategies and tools are universal. You can use them with any grade level or content area for

Grades K–12. In fact, the Redirect Behavior Model can be used outside of the classroom as well. It can be used in meetings, with parents, administrators, customer service, or significant others.

Once I had established the Positive Behavior Expectations, the students were very well versed in what and how to conduct themselves. Along with the Redirect Behavior Model and Voice-Movement-Task Model, students were more aware of their behavior and began to self-regulate. I felt like I was stealing money from the district! It was too easy. I was truly the guide on the side. I was the facilitator. I was a teacher!

Here are some last pieces of advice to guide you through your journey in classroom management.

Humor

Remember your sense of humor. Whether you are teaching elementary or college level, your students are still growing and developing as human beings. They are going to make mistakes, and sometimes it is more than okay to laugh with them and start over. They will say and do things that will make you chuckle, only to remind you that they are human beings. Sometimes you need to stop taking yourself so seriously. Yes, there's pressure to increase test scores; yes, you will be expected to be a teacher, mom, dad, counselor, referee, and task master, but give yourself a break. Have some fun! There is no need to go to work angry or uptight. It is much easier to go with the flow.

For the perfectionists out there, be kind to yourself. It's great that you have high expectations; just be careful you don't lose sight of what's best for your students. Keep your ideas and solutions simple. And learn to let things go. Do I hear a "Let It Go" from *Frozen*? Sing that song periodically, then take a day off and go to a spa!

Relationships, Trust, and Respect

I'm sure we can all agree that relationships are the absolute key to success in having a well-managed classroom. Taking the time to know and understand your students can have a powerful effect on student achievement. It provides a foundation in which to work on having an inclusive, safe learning environment.

Relationships, trust, and respect are pillars for establishing a safe and well-managed classroom. All of the CALM Management methods involve these characteristics, which are foundational to building a positive classroom community.

Communication

All of the CALM Management strategies are centered on building a community based on trust and respect. If used on a consistent basis, they will have a calming effect on the students as well as the teacher. Students will mirror their leader's mannerisms or leadership style. If you are a teacher who tends to raise your voice or send a student out of the room, the students will adjust and follow your lead. They will use a louder tone of voice, become easily agitated, and mimic how you handle pressure. Take your role as leader seriously. They are watching and learning how you respond to every situation. Remain calm and in control of your emotions and you will be able to effectively influence people.

Patience

CALM Management is not a fast-food fix. It isn't an instant antidote that will relieve all symptoms of disruptive behavior. Rather, it's a process. It takes time to establish your expectations and have students be able to carry out the Positive Behavior Expectations at a high level. The Redirect Behavior Model is uncomfortable at first. In particular, Phase I can sound scripted, but with practice it will become a part of your speech. Phase I will sound like you are having a conversation.

Behavior and Content

Approach teaching behavior as you would teaching content. Some students will grasp your behavior expectations without much prompting or teaching, some will need a little more practice, and yet others may need a great deal of time in and out of the classroom to teach the appropriate behavior. It is not different with content. You adjust your teaching according to their skills and knowledge.

You may use gradual release to teach content; employ the same technique with behavior. At first, the teacher is at the center of every teaching moment in the classroom. As students progress and become proficient with their behavior, you will gradually release the control over to them. They are held accountable; they begin to self-correct and make better choices. Just as you give choices with content, you will give choices with their behavior.

Choices

CALM Management is based on choices. You can't make anybody do anything they do not want to do. But if you offer choices it diminishes the power struggle and empowers the students to make good choices. The Redirect Behavior Model is based on giving choices. It is key in transferring the responsibility from the teacher to the student by allowing them to have time to make their decision. By transferring the power of choice to the student, it helps teachers not to take things personally when a student is disruptive. It reminds teachers that it is the student's choice—whatever choice they make will have a consequence, whether it is a positive or a negative consequence.

One Last Collaborative Group Activity

Garage Sale Project

When I was teaching seventh-grade math, we had a wonderful STEM department. It would build and program robots that could move, carry, or race around any obstacle. The STEM team was fortunate to have a large grant to fund these projects. It was an outstanding opportunity for our top students.

However, things were different for my math class. Even though my students were extremely bright and worthy of working on a STEM project, unlike the

STEM team I didn't have the expensive components to assemble robots. I felt like I was cheating my class. Only the top students were able to engage with the robots in the STEM team. I didn't think that was fair. I didn't want lack of funding to prevent my math students from having those rich experiences.

I asked my students, "What do you do after school? What do you do in your spare time? What do you do on the weekends?" I received the same low-toned utterances of "not much," "watch TV," "video games," "I don't know," "nothing." I asked if they ever took apart a radio—if they ever built a bike ramp or a fort. They were silent. I told them that when I was their age or a little younger I converted a lawn mower into a go-cart. They couldn't stop laughing. It was a push mower with no brakes, so I guess that would be pretty funny to imagine. I told them how I took apart radios and put them back together. I built forts, tree houses, and pig pens. You name it, I tried to build it. I wanted to offer my students the same opportunities I had had to create and build. And then it hit me: I didn't have a robotics kit when I was young, but I did have old appliances and car parts. This inspired me to go to garage sales and purchase radios, hair dryers, toaster ovens, vacuums—anything that had a motor and electrical parts.

We began to create our own, authentic STEM projects on a minimal budget with garage sale items!

Description

The Garage Sale Project is a challenging project that gives students an authentic, real-world experience working in collaborative groups to apply their math and science skills. It addresses the long-asked question: "When are we ever going to use this math and science?"

Students learn to assess their progress and think critically to solve problems. Each team is given a different engineering problem and a different appliance to solve the problem. The students employ the engineering design process. This entails: (1) defining the problem, (2) doing background research,

(3) brainstorming solutions, (4) choosing the best solution, (5) building a prototype, and (6) testing and redesign.

The team consisted not only of students but also community leaders working with them to employ new and innovative solutions. Experts were engineers, architects, construction managers, and computer programmers. The level of involvement depended on the relationship with the professionals. Some served as advisers, or one-day speakers regarding a particular topic; others served on a panel of judges for the final project presentation.

Collaborative Grouping

Collaborative grouping, constructing new knowledge, and applying the new knowledge to solve real-world situations are critical to student achievement (Madill, Ciccocioppo, Stewin, et al., 2004). The National Research Council (2011) stated the overall goal for STEM education is to prepare students for postsecondary fields of study and with 21st-century working skills. Project-based learning provides students with an opportunity to engage in authentic learning opportunities that investigate current problems and solutions. Students are able to resolve an issue by working in a collaborative team environment and applying critical thinking and problem-solving skills. The Garage Sale Project uses kitchen appliances, radios, and toys purchased in a garage sale to create an authentic learning experience to solve real-world problems by applying basic math concepts to new and innovative solutions.

Alternative Modifications

Each quarter we had a different project. Often the project ideas were student driven. I gave them parameters and they would design a solution. Each team was required to note the theories and algorithms it utilized. Here are some of our project ideas:

- Build robots.
- Construct a replica of a building(s) in the community and improve it with "green" solutions.
- Take an appliance apart and put it back together, developing and using algorithms.

- Find a need and design a solution—e.g., improved elevator shaft, soccer ball retriever, bike lock.

- Design a "car" for racing.

Note that students will often be excited and may begin to bring materials from home for the project. This is fine; however, indicate that doing so is optional, not a requirement. I also checked with parents for their approval with the appliance the student brought from home. I wanted to make sure the student wasn't bringing a hair dryer the family still used!

Logistics

Time

Students were able to work on the projects after all completion of their daily work. This project motivated the students to stay on task in order to be able to work on the project. The students followed the Positive Behavior Expectations for small-group work behavior.

The project due dates varied according to the scale of the project, the available materials, and time during class. There were particular moments of the year when we were not able to dedicate as much time to the project as others. Conversely, sometimes we were able to dedicate a class period per week to work on the project. Keeping due dates following 2–6 weeks will maintain student interest and motivation.

Assessment

The students were required to maintain a journal of all their ideas, algorithms, theories, and notes. The journal served as an assessment of their growth and learning. Rubrics were utilized for evaluating group work, journals, presentation, and the final project. Peer evaluations and self-reflections were implemented on a weekly basis.

Experts

Experts were community members who were employed in the field of study. The level of their involvement varied. This was on a voluntary basis, so the time they offered was at their discretion. The volunteers would present information regarding specific ideas or needs the students may encounter. They served as mentors and would support the team face to face or via email or texting. Some volunteers would serve on a panel to judge the final project. The experts varied regarding occupation. We involved doctors, engineers, landscapers, construction managers, electricians, cafeteria servers, chefs, computer programmers, building engineers, waiters/waitresses, and day-care providers.

Presentation

Team members were required to present their projects. They had to state the need, details regarding their project design, the team development, leadership, how the project solved the problem, and a reflection. Each member of the team was required to deliver a portion of the presentation. The presentations improved with each project.

Research

A research component required students to look up past projects that paralleled their design. For instance, how was the design of a specific building able to withstand winds of up to 100 mph? Students were able to apply mathematical formulas to their design based on past projects that were similar in structure.

Involving Multiple Disciplines

The project has the capacity to involve the core courses. Science and math were the center of the projects. However, English/language arts and social sciences could also contribute to the project. The social sciences could address past and present historical figures, architecture, engineering, global environmental effects, economics, and political impact. English/language arts could address appropriate methods to write the journal entries, research paper, and presentation format.

Where Do We Go From Here?

As educators, we meet the learning needs of our students. We adjust the method of delivery to ensure all students are able to comprehend the material in multiple forms of learning. We need to continue this philosophy with our teachers: adjust our delivery of professional development to meet the needs of all teachers, make a more inclusive approach for ESL, STEM, novice, and veteran teachers alike. Maybe we should look at professional learning communities with varying levels of choices and content areas. If a veteran teacher has a good grasp on classroom management, they may benefit from areas of developing their leadership skills, whether they want to remain in the classroom or begin their journey into administration. Classroom management is such a wide area, with the greatest impact on learners; we cannot take this subject lightly. Too often we dismiss classroom management with the philosophy of "throw the new teachers into the fire—that's how I learned." This is a dangerous ideology to endorse.

The challenges teachers face today are complex and multilayered. Yet teachers are extremely adept at changing with the needs of the students. We have to be able to give teachers innovative strategies and methods of addressing the diverse needs of the students and teachers alike. It's a balance between teaching behavior and teaching content. With continued efforts in concentrating on implicitly teaching behavior not only in the beginning of the school year, but throughout the year, the teacher will be able to engage their students in dynamic, robust content strategies that seek to achieve a deeper understanding of the information presented. Classroom management is an absolute key in approaching the diverse learning environment. A well-managed classroom with a classroom culture that embraces diversity, appropriate behavior, and a productive work ethic will need to have student behavior working at a high level of respect. If the teacher has a positive classroom community, they can divide their time to address academic needs—extension activities, extra support for low achievers, English language learners, projects that empower students to employ and extend their critical thinking skills—all of these areas may be addressed simultaneously during class time, but only if the teacher has the behavior working at a high level.

Continuing our focus on developing students as leaders, there may be a greater transfer of the responsibility of learning onto the student. Encouraging students to take the lead, improve communication skills, and make efforts in self-regulating their behavior may lead to a more productive classroom. A greater understanding of integrating behavior and content knowledge into daily lessons may have an impact on improving learning outcomes. The need to understand how behavior and content knowledge have a parallel effect on student achievement is of great importance in understanding how to teach the whole child.

We cannot continue to dismiss the importance of developing teachers' classroom management skills. We talk at great lengths of how important it is to have a well-managed classroom, but we do not always provide professional development that addresses specific strategies that meet the diverse needs of the classroom.

Teachers need to take the lead in collaborating with one another on a local, state, national, and global level. Show the students what it means to be a collaborator with your colleagues. Show the students how you include colleagues from around the world. When you show the students that you are willing to share your thoughts, ideas, and work on projects with colleagues three states away, the students will begin to follow your lead. Establishing a community of respect and acceptance within your classroom will encourage students to initiate discourse with students of differing views.

In a perfect world, the teacher and students would be free of bias, embrace their differences, and encourage one another to be the best person they can be. Wouldn't that be great? It sounds like a pipedream, and though some may say you will never be able to attain such euphoria, why not try for it? We may not achieve the perfect classroom, but we have to keep trying.

Teaching tolerance is a complex topic that requires a strong teacher leader in every classroom. Our collective goal as teachers should focus on developing methods to promote authentic discourse. We need to be strategic in addressing how to teach students to communicate and share their ideas while maintaining a high level of respect throughout discourse. It is a multilayered issue that requires innovative thinking from the teachers and students. It is essential that teachers today promote a greater understanding and acceptance of our underserved populations.

How we do this remains a work in progress. There are opportunities for collaborative efforts, engaging thought leaders who are willing to take a risk and try new methods of addressing social issues. We cannot continue to dismiss and turn a blind eye to the diverse needs of our students. We need to be willing to work as professionals in every grade level and content area. Small and large efforts all make a difference; it is our duty to give every child an equal access to quality education.

References

Alderman, M. K. (2008). *Motivation for achievement: Possibilities for teaching and learning* (3rd ed.). New York: Routledge.

Arthur, M., Gordon, C., & Butterfield, N. (2003). *Classroom management: Creating positive learning environments*. Southbank, Victoria, Australia: Thomson.

Bandura, A. (1986). *Social foundations of thought and action*. Englewood Cliffs, NJ: Prentice Hall.

Bandura, A. (1997). *Self-efficacy: The exercise of control*. New York: W. H. Freeman.

Barton-Arwood, S., Morrow, L., Lane, K., & Jolivette, K. (2005). Project IMPROVE: Improving teachers' ability to address students' social needs. *Education and Treatment of Children*, *28*, 430–443.

Beaman, R., & Wheldall, K. (2000). Teachers' use of approval and disapproval in the classroom. *Educational Psychology*, *20*, 431–446.

Beebe-Frankenberger, M., Lane, K., Bocian, K., Gresham, F., & MacMillan, D. (2005). Students with or at risk for problem behavior: Betwixt and between teacher and parent expectations. *Preventing School Failure*, *49*(2), 10–16.

Black, R., & Walsh, L. (2009, February). Corporate Australia and schools: Forming business class alliances and networks. Seminar Series Paper 182. Melbourne, Australia: Centre for Strategic Education.

Bryan, R. R., Glynn, S. M., & Kittleson, J. M. (2011). Motivation, achievement, and advanced placement intent of high school students learning science. *Science Education*, *95*(6), 1049–1065.

Clunies-Ross, P., Little, E., & Kienhuis, M. (2008). Self-reported and actual use of proactive and reactive classroom management strategies and their relationship with teacher stress and student behaviour. *Educational Psychology*, *28*(6), 693–710.

Corbell, K., Booth, S., & Reiman, A. (2010). The commitment and retention intentions of traditional and alternative licensed math and science beginning teachers. *Journal of Curriculum and Instruction*, *4*(1), 50–69.

Cuddy, A. (2015). *Presence: Bringing your boldest self to your biggest challenges*. New York: Little, Brown and Company.

Deci, E. L., & Ryan, R. M. (1985). *Intrinsic motivation and self-determination in human behavior*. New York: Plenum.

Deci, E. L., & Ryan, R. M. (2000). The "what" and "why" of goal pursuits: Human needs and the self-determination of behavior. *Psychological Inquiry*, *11*(4), 227–268.

Deci, E. L., Vallerand, R. J., Pelletier, L. G., & Ryan, R. M. (1991). Motivation and education: The self-determination perspective. *Educational Psychologist, 26,* 325–346. doi:10.1080/00461520.1991.9653137

Evertson, C. M., Emmer, E. T., & Worsham. M. E. (2006). *Classroom management for elementary teachers* (7th ed.). Boston, MA: Pearson Allyn & Bacon.

Fernley, S. (2011). What is time to teach. Retrieved from http://www .timetoteachnow.com/index.htm

Forness, S. R. (2005). The pursuit of evidence-based practice in special education for children with emotional or behavioral disorders. *Behavioral Disorders, 30,* 311–330.

Harvey, S. T., & Evans, I. M. (2003) Teachers' emotional skills, as required in the classroom. *Journal of Educational Research, 46,* 1–15.

Ingersoll, R., Merrill, L., & Stuckey, D. (2014, April). Seven trends: The transformation of the teaching force. *CPRE Research Reports.* Retrieved from http://www.cpre.org/7trends

Institute of Education Sciences. (2012). *Reducing behavior problems in the elementary school classroom.* National Center for Education Evaluation and Regional Assistance. Retrieved from http://ies.ed.gov/ncee/wwc/pdf/practice_guides/ behavior_pg_092308.pdf

Jones, A. C. (2008). The effects of out-of-class support on student satisfaction and motivation to learn. *Communication Education, 57,* 373–388. doi:10.1080/03634520801968830

Jones, J. (2014). Best practices in providing culturally responsive interventions. In P. L. Harrison & A. Thomas (Eds.), *Best practices in school psychology* (6th ed., pp. 49–60). Bethesda, MD: National Association of School Psychologists.

Kaff, M. S., Zabel, R. H., & Milham, M. (2007).Revisiting cost-benefit relationships of behavior management strategies: What special educators say about usefulness, intensity, and effectiveness. *Preventing School Failure, 51*(2), 35–45.

Knight, J. (2014). *Focus on teaching: Using video for high-impact instruction.* Thousand Oaks, CA: Corwin.

Kyriacou, C., Avramidis, E., Hoie, H., Stephens, P., & Hultgren, A. (2007). The development of student teachers' views on pupil misbehavior during an initial teacher training programme in England and Norway. *Journal of Education for Teaching, 33,* 293–307.

Lannie, A., & McCurdy, B. (2007). Preventing disruptive behavior in the urban classroom: Effects of the good behavior game on student and teacher behavior. *Education and Treatment of Children, 30*(1), 85–98.

La Paro, K. M, & Pianta, R. C. (2003). *CLASS: Classroom Assessment Scoring System.* Charlottesville: University of Virginia Press.

Lentfer, V. S., & Franks, B. A. (2015). Effects of training in the Redirect Behavior Model on pre-service teachers' self-efficacy in classroom management. *Journal of Curriculum, Teaching, Learning, and Leadership in Education, 1*(9).

Madill, H. M., Ciccocioppo, A., Stewin, L. L., et al. (2004). The potential to develop a career in sciences: Young women's issues and their implications for careers guidance initiatives. *International Journal for the Advancement of Counselling, 26*, 1. doi:10.1023/B:ADCO.0000021546.17402.5b

Marzano, R. J. (2010). High expectations for all. *Educational Leadership, 68*(1), 82–84.

Marzano, R. J., Marzano, J. S., & Pickering, D. J. (2003). *Classroom management that works*. Alexandria, VA: Association for Supervision and Curriculum Development.

Maton, K., & Salem, D. (1995). Organizational characteristics of empowering in community settings: A multiple case study approach. *American Journal of Community Psychology, 23*, 631–656.

McKinney, S., Campbell-Whately, G., & Kea, C. (2005). Managing student behavior in urban classrooms: The role of teacher ABC assessments. *Clearing House, 79*(1), 16–20.

McKown, C., & Weinstein, R. (2008). Teacher expectations, classroom context, and the achievement gap. *Journal of School Psychology, 46*(3), 235–261. doi:1O.1016/j.jsp.2007.05.001

Melnick, S., & Meister, D. (2008). A comparison of beginning and experienced teachers' concerns. *Educational Research Quarterly, 31*(3), 39–56.

Mitchell, A., & Arnold, M. (2004). Behavior management skills as predictors of retention among south Texas special educators. *Journal of Instructional Psychology, 31*, 214–219.

National Research Council. (2011). *Successful K–12 STEM education: Identifying effective approaches in science, technology, engineering, and mathematics*. Committee on Highly Successful Science Programs for K–12 Science Education, Board on Science Education and Board on Testing and Assessment, Division of Behavioral and Social Sciences and Education. Washington, DC: The National Academies Press.

Neary, E. M., & Eyberg, S. M. (2002). Management of disruptive behavior in young children. *Infants and Young Children, 14*(4), 53–67.

Niesyn, M. (2009). Strategies for success: Evidence-based instructional practices for students with emotional and behavioral disorders. *Preventing School Failure, 53*, 227–233.

Nottingham, J., & Nottingham, J. (2017). *Challenging learning through feedback: How to get the type, tone, and quality of feedback right every time*. Thousand Oaks, CA: Corwin.

Osher, D., Sprague, J., Weissberg, R. P., Axelrod, J., Keenan, S., Kendziora, K., & Zins, J. E. (2007). A comprehensive approach to promoting social, emotional, and academic growth in contemporary schools. In A. Thomas & J. Grimes (Eds.), *Best practices in school psychology* (Vol. 5, 5th ed., pp. 1263–1278). Bethesda, MD: National Association of School Psychologists.

Perkins, D., & Zimmerman, M. (1995) Empowerment theory, research, and application. *American Journal of Community Psychology, 23*, 569–580.

Peters, J. (2012). Are they ready? Final year pre-service teachers' learning about managing student behaviour. *Australian Journal of Teacher Education, 37*, 18–42. doi:10.14221/ajte.2012v37n9.2

Ratcliffe, N. J., Carroll, K. L., & Hunt, G. H. (2014). Teacher retreating: The little known behavior that impacts teaching and learning. *Education, 135*(2), 169–176.

Schunk, D. H., & Usher, E. L. (2013). Barry Zimmerman's theory of self-regulated learning. In H. Bembenutty, T. J. Cleary, & A. Kitsantas (Eds.), *Applications of self-regulated learning across diverse disciplines: A tribute to Barry J. Zimmerman* (pp. 1–28). Charlotte, NC: Information Age.

Shook, A. (2009). *Preservice teacher preparation for managing behavior problems: Preventing and managing problem behaviors in the general education classroom.* Bean-Bassin, Mauritius: VDM Verlag.

Smart, J., & Brent, I. (2010). A grounded theory of behavior management strategy selection, implementation, and perceived effectiveness reported by first-year elementary teachers. *Elementary School Journal, 110*, 567–584. doi:10.1086/651196

Smith, S. C., Lewis, T. J., & Stormont, M. (2011). *The effectiveness of two universal behavioral supports for children with externalizing behavior in Head Start classrooms. Positive Behavior Interventions, 13*, 133–143.

Spreitzer, G. (1995). An empirical test of a comprehensive model of intrapersonal empowerment in the workplace. *American Journal of Community Psychology, 23*, 601–630.

Stormont, M. A., & Reinke, W. (2009). The importance of precorrective statements and behavior-specific praise and strategies to increase their use. *Beyond Behavior, 18*(3), 26–32.

Stormont, M. A., Smith, S. C., & Lewis, T. J. (2007). Teacher implementation of precorrection and praise statements in Head Start classrooms as a component of a program-wide system of positive behavior support. *Journal of Behavioral Education, 16*, 280–290.

Sugai, G., Horner, R. H., & McIntosh, K. (2008). Best practices in developing a broad scale system of support for school-wide positive behavior support. In A. Thomas & J. P. Grimes (Eds.), *Best practices in school psychology* (Vol. 3, pp. 765–780). Bethesda, MD: National Association of School Psychologists.

Thomas, D. R., Becker, W. C., & Armstrong, M. (1968). Production and elimination of disruptive classroom behavior by systematically varying teacher's behavior. *Journal of Applied Behavior Analysis, 1*, 35–45.

Tillery, A. D., Varjas, K., Meyers, J., & Collins, A. S. (2009). General education teachers' perceptions of behavior management and intervention strategies. *Journal of Positive Behavior Interventions, 12*(2), 86–102. doi:10.1177/1098300708330879

Westling, D. L. (2010). Teachers and challenging behavior: Knowledge, views, and practices. *Remedial and Special Education, 31*(1), 48–63. doi:10.1177/0741932508327466

Zimmerman, B. J. (2008). Goal setting: A key proactive source of academic self-regulation. In D. H. Schunk & B. J. Zimmerman (Eds.), *Motivation and self-regulated learning: Theory, research, and applications* (pp. 267–295). New York: Erlbaum.

Zimmerman, M. (1995). Psychological empowerment: Issues and illustrations. *American Journal of Community Psychology, 23*, 581–600.

Zirpoli, T. J. (2008). *Behavior management: Applications for teachers.* Upper Saddle River, NJ: Pearson.

Index

A SAGE Publishing Company

Helping educators make the greatest impact

CORWIN HAS ONE MISSION: to enhance education through intentional professional learning.

We build long-term relationships with our authors, educators, clients, and associations who partner with us to develop and continuously improve the best evidence-based practices that establish and support lifelong learning.

The Association for Middle Level Education is dedicated to improving the educational experiences of all students ages 10 to 15 by providing vision, knowledge, and resources to educators and leaders.

Confident Teachers, Inspired Learners

No matter where you are in your professional journey, Corwin aims to ease the many demands teachers face on a daily basis with accessible strategies that benefit ALL learners. Through research-based, high-quality content we offer practical guidance on a wide range of topics, including curriculum planning, learning frameworks, classroom design and management, and much more. Our books, videos, consulting, and online resources were developed by renowned educators and designed for easy implementation that will provide tangible results for you *and* your students.

LISA WESTMAN

Full of step-by-step guidance, this book shows you how to build collaborative student-teacher relationships and incorporate student voice and choice in the process of planning for student-driven differentiation.

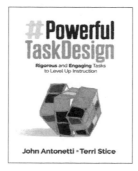

JOHN ANTONETTI AND TERRI STICE

This book will teach you to use the Powerful Task Rubric for Designing Student Work to analyze, design, and refine engaging tasks of learning.

CAROL PELLETIER RADFORD

This newly revised edition prepares new teachers for the rigors and expectations of the classroom. It includes mentor-teacher strategies, a flexible twelve-month curriculum, companion website, and more!

SERENA PARISER

This handy guide offers 50 proven best practices for managing today's classroom, complete with just-in-time tools and relatable teacher-to-teacher anecdotes and advice.

GRAVITY GOLDBERG

In *Teach Like Yourself*, Gravity Goldberg applies ideas from fields of psychology, education, and science to name five key habits involving core beliefs, practice, relationships, professional growth, and one's whole self.

HEATHER WOLPERT-GAWRON

Based on over 1000 nationwide student surveys, these 10 deep engagement strategies help you implement achievement-based cooperative learning. Includes video and a survey sample.

corwin.com

CORWIN

N188C